LIVING TOGETHER:

An Ethnography of a Retirement Hotel

Marea Teski

University Press of America™

To: Velma Osborne Panares, my mother

and

Krzysztof Stefan Teski, my husband.

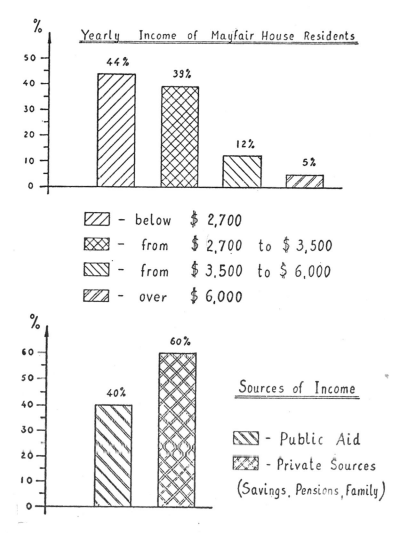

Yearly Income of Mayfair House Residents

44% 39% 12% 5%

▨ — below $ 2,700
▨ — from $ 2,700 to $ 3,500
▨ — from $ 3,500 to $ 6,000
▨ — over $ 6,000

Sources of Income

60% 40%

▨ — Public Aid
▨ — Private Sources
(Savings, Pensions, Family)

TABLE OF CONTENTS

ACKNOWLEDGEMENTS

A true listing of acknowledgements would have to go back to the beginning of my educational process. Therefore, I shall limit mine to those people who directly aided in the research and writing of this book. First of all, my great thanks go to Conrad Arensberg of Columbia University who first interested me in the concept of community and community studies. David Bidney of Indiana University turned my atten tion to the possibilities of anthropological field studies in complex society. Anya Royce of Indiana University encouraged my interest in the elderly long before they were a fashionable subject. Special thanks should go to Helena Lopata of Loyola Univer- sity and her mother the late Eileen Znaniecki for their special knowledge and help in the community I studied. Professor Lopata was a constant source of fresh approaches and new ideas during the re- search period. Diagrams and graphs are the work of my husband Krzysztof Teski and the manuscript pre- paration the work of Margaret Roche. I wish to ex- press my deepest thanks to all of these individuals. I shall not forget their help.

INTRODUCTION

The elderly in America are a category of citizens whose distinctive social patterns, roles and needs must be better understood and more fully considered in our society. This work is a study of old people living in a retirement hotel. It focuses upon social interaction, social structure and the shared meaning created in the group. Observation at the hotel was carried out over a period of nine months. The purpose of the study is to improve our understanding of the needs of the elderly by describing ways in which a fairly stable social structure and a shared reality are built among people who have spent a lifetime in other different communities before coming to the retirement community. We will try to understand the effects of both participation and non-participation in the retirement community on the residents.

In terms of the larger goals of Anthropology, the study provides an opportunity for the use of the intensive, long term methods of observation particular to this discipline to focus on a problem which is significant in the society at large as well as in the small community of observation. The problem is that of the relations and distribution of power between a younger, more powerful and prosperous group and an older less prosperous and less powerful group. In the retirement hotel, the less prosperous group is represented by the residents and the younger group is represented by the staff. The monopolization of power by the staff and the importance of "acting like staff" for residents who want access to the small amount of power available to them are important indicators of the association of power with relative youth. In many ways the relations between older and younger in contemporary society are clarified through observation in the microcosm of the retirement hotel.

The study focuses on four main questions: 1)What is the nature of the community which we find in a one building retirement hotel? Is it one community or many? How does it hold together? 2) What is the social structure here and how are power and status positions achieved and recognized? 3) How is shared meaning achieved and maintained? and 4) What are the main problems of this type of artificially created community?

In order to find an appropriate unit for study and the answering of these questions I wanted to find a community in which most of the residents were elderly. After considering the possibilities of retirement villages, largely elderly neighborhoods, towns where the elderly congregate in Florida and California, it began to be obvious that the type of "Life World" and intense and intimate social interaction which would be most fruitful and interesting could best be found in a one-building retirement hotel. Here it would be possible, in the time of a few months to talk at length with most of the residents and to attend almost all of the social events. Further, it was suggested that a hotel with a communal dining room would be best since, at least three times a day, almost all of the residents could be seen together. Because the focus of research was to be normal social life among fairly healthy older people, hotels with hospital or nursing home facilities were not considered. Mayfair House with its insistence that it is a hotel for the "active" retired person seemed ideal.

The hotel is isolated from the community outside insofar as it is a single building only for "old folks" and yet it is part of a city neighborhood, offering a chance to get out into the life of the city to residents who are able. A bus to the main shopping area of the city stops just outside the hotel, and small shops in the neighborhood provide for immediate needs. An interesting situation developed when the corporation which owns the hotel became involved in supporting a bill which would make the hotel neighbor-hood a "dry" one. It was felt that the absence of liquor stores might help cut down the high crime rate and make the area safer for the elderly residents. To the great surprise of the staff, the idea was un-popular with the residents. They too want a safe neighborhood, but too many of them also loved the convenience of just having to go next door for a bottle of something! The residents value being in a city neighborhood with the shops close at hand.

Having chosen a unit for study, I determined to use the traditional anthropological method of partici-pant observation and set about trying to arrange that. The administration of the hotel, although they wanted a study done of the facility, were very concerned about

strangers "disturbing" the residents. Many of them.
had been interviewed for sociological surveys, but
no long term study with a constant observer had ever
been done at Mayfair. The staff was unwilling for me
to present myself as a researcher, but suggested that
it would be acceptable for me to be a kind of staff
aide - helping with whatever was necessary to do. As
I had a car, I could be useful giving people rides
when they needed to go somewhere. I was to be an
all-purpose helper.

Actually, the presence of an observer at Mayfair
made the staff uneasy from the beginning until the end
of the research period, although they said constantly
how glad they were to have people taking an interest
in the social life of the elderly. They wanted, at
first, to present me with the "guest version" of life
at the hotel, but as in the case of the houseguest
who stays too long, social pretenses finally had to
be relaxed and I was let in on the "real" version of
Mayfair life. Once it was clear that I was cooperating
in reality maintenance and not being too disruptive,
I became rather invisible and was usually ignored by
staff.

The first problem was to make contact with as
many residents as possible and for this purpose the
dining room was ideal. The 350 residents eat each
meal in two sittings. Unless they are ill, each
resident appears at least once or twice in the dining
room every day. Announcements are made here and it is
the only room large enough to hold half of all the
residents at one time.

At first I was given the task of making the
"table checks" for two meals a day. This consists of
checking the table before the meal to make sure that
bread, salt, pepper, sugar, etc. are there and going
around from table to table during the meal asking how
people liked the food, what their requests are, and so
forth. At each table I introduced myself as a new
"helper" and invited everyone to come into the little
office I had been given to talk. After several days
of doing this I came to know most of the residents
by sight and they also knew me. People began coming
to my office to talk about everything under the sun,
and soon I was well acquainted with about 100 people.
During the research I came to know about 150 people
really well, and to know all of the others by sight. I
began to know the habits even of those to whom I had

never spoken. Only one or two residents ever questioned why I was there. Most of them accept new people
in the environment as a matter of course and began to
see ways in which I could be useful.

I attended almost every social event, and although
I was conspicuous at first, after about a month no
one bothered to ask why I was attending. At first I
was expected to take an active part in events as the
staff always do. Later, after I had spent weeks just
sitting there appearing to watch but not intervene,
no one expected me to take a directive role. I had
established that this was not to be my approach, and
soon things began to happen almost as if I had not
been there.

Very soon I was extremely busy taking people
around the city as well as attending all of the social
events. I visited people in·hospitals and took others
to visit sick friends. I made numerous phone calls
to Social Security and Public Aid and took many residents to these offices.

I made some use of questionnaires trying to find
out how many people a resident spoke with each day,
how often children came to visit, how often the administrator was consulted about problems, and other
questions relating to life-style at the hotel.
Questionnaires were not new to the residents; they had
been interviewed many times by sociologists and
sociology students from local universities. However,
I decided to abandon this method when I found I was
getting more accurate information through my observations and through the constant casual conversations
I was having with the residents. When I first used
the questionnaire I had already been at the hotel
for three months, and it might have been more successful had I used it before people knew me so well. Many
felt that they knew me too well to be "interviewed"
and tended to talk about things other than the questions. Therefore they were not serious about the
questionnaires and used interview time to try to tell
me what was on their minds rather than staying with
the questions.

In my observations I tried to concentrate on
two things 1) events and 2) conversations. Events
are of two kinds, the planned and the unplanned. The
planned event would be, for example, a birthday party,
while the unplanned could be someone drunk appearing

in the hall of the dining room. Conversations are
also of various kinds. They are divided into two
basic categories: conversations which comment on
events and general conversations which deal with life
and "the way things are".

A conversation is, of course, a kind of event,
but for this study an event is defined as a happening
which includes more than conversation. It involves
actions and conversation too, although it may be
actions alone. Details of events were recorded
in written notes and I tried to write down conversations verbatum soon after they occurred. There was
not time to think about these events and conversations.
I simply wrote them down for later reflection. This
was, in the end, a good method because I had no time
for editing and writing down what I thought was
important and leaving out other things.

My approach to observation and data collection
was phenomenological -- it was concerned with accurate
description of what was said and done. I concentrated
on particular occurences in order to formulate an
expanded description of both the social and the per-
ceptual reality at Mayfair House. I feel that this
method was extremely effective because of the economy
of initial assumptions and the lack of distortion in
using as far as possible non-selective observation.
As I have said, I was interested in certain problems-
the relations between old and younger people and the
building of a meaningful life by the old when they
have left the familiar millieu of the earlier
part of life. The phenomenological method of observation yielded a great deal of information which can
be used to improve understanding in both these areas.
At the end of the research period I had a mass of
descriptive material about events and conversations.
None of it proved to be unimportant. From this material
emerged a distinct life world and social hicrarchy
characteristic of Mayfair House as well as some new
insight into the effects of powerlessness, loneliness,
and isolation in all human beings and in this society
in particular.

CHAPTER I

THE REALITY OF THE RETIREMENT HOTEL

In many ways a retirement hotel is a world within a world, a society within a society. Mayfair House, the retirement hotel where I spent nine months in observation is such a world. It is a once elegant hotel in a now deteriorated neighborhood in the city of Chicago. Mayfair House belongs to a corporation which owns 19 hotels in this urban area, all of which are used as retirement facilities. Mayfair House is not the true name of the hotel, nor are any of the personal names I have used the true names of the residents. All names of places and groups within the hotel have also been changed. About 350 men and women, mainly of working class or lower middle class background, (with a few notable exceptions) make their home here. There are Jews, Roman Catholics and Protestants in approximately equal numbers. There are immigrants from most of the countries of Europe, one gentleman of Japanese origin, and "typical" Americans whose ancestors have been in the United States for generations. The residents range in age from about 51 to 91 and it would be hard to imagine a more varied group. There are an almost exactly equal number of men and women.

What then is the reality of the world at Mayfair House? It is a world in which people unlike one another are attempting to find community and meaning in old age. It is the scene of their building and their struggle. There is a formal pattern of assembly and disperal based upon gathering in the dining room for three meals a day. Through time and through communication between staff and residents and among residents a structure of reality or everyday life has been built. In conversation, activities, and events this reality is maintained and modified through time.

Like all everyday worlds, and perhaps even more so than some, the sense of reality of things at Mayfair House is threatened from time to time. The fact that the residents come from so many different backgrounds and are, as elderly people, approaching death, are important considerations in thinking about the problem of reality maintenance.

> The precariousness of every such world is revealed each time men forget or doubt the reality-denying dreams of "madness" and, most importantly, each time they consciously encounter death. Every human society is, in

> the last resort, men banded to gether in the
> face of death... (Berger 1969:51)

Death, doubt, the non-participant in social life, and
the stranger are all sources of possible feelings
of unreality. All of these sources had to be dealt
with by the residents of Mayfair House. The population
at the hotel is constantly changing because of the
arrival of new residents and the departure of old
residents to hospitals, nursing homes or through death
This means that there are always strangers about who
must adjust to the reality of everyday life here before it is their reality.

Also there are always present some residents who
do not participate in social life. The fact that they
are often present at the scene of social events, but
not participating in them is distressing to residents
The sense of unreality and disturbance is produced
by the fact that some people are there who are not
at all involved in what is going on. Goffman (1963)
discusses this in terms of the types of individual
involvement which are not allowable in a social
situation. One of the types is that of being physically present but not involved or involvable in the
action which is taking place.

A number of Mayfair residents are unable or unwilling to take part in social interaction. Yet,
they are almost always physically present, especially
on the more important social occasions. This creates
a great deal of discomfort among other residents who
find it upsetting no matter how long they have lived
at the hotel. They feel that, in the eyes of any
stranger or visitor, the presence of these individual
would cast doubt upon their own credibility as respon
sible members of society.

Doubt of the "realness" of the world of everyday
life at Mayfair was expressed often by the rebels
among the residents, sometimes by new residents and
sometimes by old residents who had "seen everything."
The fact that most of the lives of the residents had
been spent in other settings gave them a basis for
comparison. Mr. Chupp, a forthright and verbal
resident was leaving the hotel after several years
to take a small room of his own near his children.
He said: "I'm going to be lonely, maybe, but I've
offered my services to my son as a permanent baby
sitter. I get irritated, but I love those kids and

2

I know how to take care of them. It's more of a life than sitting around here waiting for the next meal. I know I'll miss my friends here, but I want to be in the real world even if its harder."

Mr. Chupp felt that, in comparison with the life he had led before, the life at Mayfair was not "real" enough to make it worth his time to remain here. Doubts such as his arise when people compare their former lives to the one they are leading at present. This is particularly true when the resident regards the younger years as the happier ones. The more a resident is involved with the past the less likely his life and involvements at the hotel are likely to be considered "real." In contrast, Mrs. Gubala regards her time at Mayfair as the best time of her life. She says: "All my life I had nothing but work, work, work. I had not time for friends - it was all the time work. Now I got time and I have friends. If I feel tired I can rest. Now I have fun."

In spite of problems and differences of opinion, there is a common everyday reality at the hotel which is shared by a majority of the residents. It is a reality of common experiences, common problems and a common environment. Living in this common environment, the residents establish social life and the social life has meaning for them. There is also a temporal element. Although the residents have come from different pasts, they share a mutual present. Shutz, using certain concepts from Bergson, sees the present as being shared through communication.

By the We-relation, thus established, we both... he addressing himself to me, and I, listening to him,...are living in our mutual vivid present, directed toward the thought to be realized in and by the communication process. We grow older together. (1970:207)

Many of the Mayfair residents are communicating and sharing a common life-world. They are "growing older together". Insofar as some residents are not, for various reasons, communicating and sharing a present with others, they will appear to the observer to be isolated and will express feelings of loneliness and isolation.

There is a life world at Mayfair, a shared reality which can be described by most of the residents

who also share evaluations of the world perceived.
Isolates are often surprised to find that they are
considered to be part of the community. Some "loners"
who were ill and received cards in the hospital feel
differently about the hotel upon their return and
attempt to socialize more.

Through communication among the residents there
is constant building and rebuilding of the life world
of the hotel. What are the forces which may fragment
this reality for the individual? We have considered
some threats to the reality of the life world in a
social sense, from the point of view of the group.
Now we will turn to the individual and describe some
of the pressures which may act upon him and may bring
him to the point where he is considered a threat to
the group as a structured social unit and as a life
world.

Because of the variety of backgrounds of the
residents, they have brought with them a huge constellation of life worlds which must somehow be
resolved in the communal experience at Mayfair House.
Each resident has past years of living in a certain
segment in society which impinge on the present experience. As part of the larger society the hotel
has many elements which will be familiar to a new
resident, but it also has new elements, a distinctive
social structure and customs which will not be familia
These must be learned and the individual must find
a place for himself in the social scheme of things.
If they are learned the new resident will become part
of a new group, if not the individual will retain
perceptions and orientations from earlier life. If
a person remains oriented to groups and structures
from the past he will be isolated in the new situation
and his isolation will assign him a negative social
status position in the new context of the hotel. We
can say that there is a real difference in how "real"
the life at Mayfair is to various residents. The
degree to which they enter the new life world is
dependent upon how well their past life has prepared
them to accept the possibility and desirability of
situational change.

However, the life world of the hotel exists and
must be dealt with in some way or another by everyone
who comes to live here. In trying to determine the
factors which separate residents from one another in

4

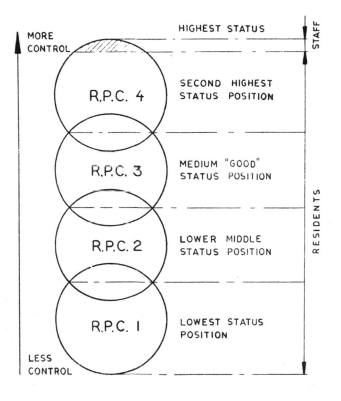

FIGURE 1

"STATUS & REALITY
PARTICIPATION CIRCLES (R.P.C.)"

their feelings, it became apparent that, although
there was indeed an objective shared life world
here, there were vast differences in breadth of participation in that world. Different individuals were
concerned with different segments of experience in the
life world of the hotel. This led to the formulation
of the idea of the "reality participation circle" as
a means of identifying the breadth of any given
individuals involvement in the social life and environment surrounding all of the residents at Mayfair House.
The reality participation circle simply refers to the
extent to which the individual is involved in the
life world - as expressed by that individual's
actions and conversations. The mental patient who
spends his days concentrating on crumbs from his
breakfast toast is in many ways part of the life world
of the institution in which he lives. It is the
narrowness of his circle of attention and others
response to their perception of this narrowness which
cuts him off from social interaction. *(See Figure 1)*

Thus, at Mayfair House we find individuals - all
part of the life world here - who have vastly different
breadths and foci of attention. Different things in
the shared life world seem important and "real" to them
Every sort of individual from the complete isolate
to the active and involved resident can be found. The
circle of participation in the shared reality is
slightly different for each. Within this broad range
of types of reality participation it is possible to
distinguish four basic categories which can describe
the range of reality participation of all of the
residents.

The following four categories describes the main
types of circles of involvement with the external
world - the world of Mayfair House and the world
beyond.

1) Individual awareness -- the physical and mental
   reality of one person - his idiosyncratic
   world view and his reactions to things around
   him.   (Obviously if too many people are
   oriented this way social life will be minimal!)

2) Small group awareness -- involvement in informal
   conversation and gossip groups.

3) Hotel social life awareness -- involvement in
   the world of the planned social program --

committees, dealings with management and staff,
working with other residents.

4) Wider world involvement -- friends, organizations,
entertainment, and communication outside the hotel.

I found over an extended period of observation that,
within the shared life world, each resident spoke and
acted with reference to one of these circles a majority
of the time. Close friendships and associations were
formed with people whose interests were within the same
circle of reality participation. Loneliness was largely
a matter of not having enough people to interact with
who were involved in a reality participation circle
similar to one's own.

Social structure and status position also have
a firm relation to the reality participation circles of
residents. Social groups were formed with reality
participation circle as a real if unmentioned criterion
of membership. Relations with staff and access to
the limited amount of power available to residents depend upon reality participation circle involvement.

Social Structure and Reality Participation Circle

Social structure is indicated at Mayfair House
through the continued daily interactions of the
residents in social situations. The main type of
social interaction here is conversation. Conversations
show reality participation circle and status position
of the speakers and confer meaning upon events. Therefore, conversation was the main focus of observation.
Actions without words and the positioning of people
and events within the hotel were important too and
were noted. However, as the main source of communication, conversation was always considered to be primary
and was given primary attention. Some days were more
days of listening -- a maze of voices and ideas --
than of observing. Thinking back over the period
of research, it is the voices even more than the scenes
which are unforgetable. No conversation was considered
too trivial to note, and later it turned out that even
when people seemed to be saying nothing they were in
fact saying things about social life, reality and the
power structure at the hotel.

As we have already noted, social postion at the
hotel is importantly tied to reality participation

6

circle. As several observers have mentioned social
life in a retirement setting is different from that
of working life. Social position is gained more
by present activities than by former job. In fact,
the retirement community may give new opportunities
for gaining a favorable social position by people
who were not happy with their positions in their
pre-retirement communities.

In the life world of Mayfair Hotel, the wider a
person's reality participation circle is the more
likely it is that that person will have a high status
position. Reality participation circle and status
position are also significantly related to the amount
of control a person is seen to have over himself and
events and how a person is treated by staff. By
and large, the residents who are respected by the
staff are also respected by their fellow residents.
Those who are ignored by staff are usually also ignored by the other residents. Individuals who are
operating within ghe wider reality participation
circles conceive of themselves as being effective
in a wider scene. They exert themselves within this
scene and often succeed in their objectives. Every
time a resident takes effective action and is seen to
do so by other residents that resident's status increases or solidifies. The residents whom the others
most respect are those who are said. to "do things".
Volunteers, committee people and "fixers" are the
ones who were named when the residents were asked
"Who are the resident leaders?" People who "contributed nothing" or "are nutty" are looked down upon
by a large proportion of the residents and are
considered negligible by the staff.

The reality participation circle of a resident
tends to determine the group or groups with which
most of his time will be spent. These social groups
are arranged in a hierarchy in the minds of most of
the residents--some having low prestige and others
having high prestige. For example, the gossip group
of the Greenhill Lounge is looked down upon by many
residents. It is thought of as being composed of
people who have "nothing better to do" and are
"out of it". On the other hand, people who are active
ly involved in the Volunteer Society and the House
Maintenance Committee are respected. They are thought
of as people who make life better for others-active
and effective people. There are some rebels who do
not agree with this system of ranking of individuals.

7

Without exception, however, these rebels saw themselves as lacking in prestige. Some blamed the hotel, some blamed themselves, and some appear not to care.

Individuals are usually classified by others in terms of their associations and also in terms of how the staff appears to treat them. The individuals who are considered to be lowest in status are those who are isolates and are also observed to be considered a bother by staff. However, there are a few isolates who have retained a good deal of respect for themselves by showing that they are clear minded and independent and that they avoided social groups out of choice. These individuals are often rebels as well - remaining constant critical strangers to the life world of Mayfair House. They are often fully aware of and involved in events of the world outside the hotel. They simply refuse to accept the world of the hotel as <u>their</u> world and although they come to terms with life here, it is never really "home".

Thus, within the nominally egalitarian society of Mayfair House, it is possible to discern a distinct hierarchy of individuals and a corresponding hierarchyof social groups. Individuals may well belong to more than one social group, but they are unlikely to belong to groups which occupy vastly different positions in the status hierarchy. Most individuals associate mainly with others with similar reality participation circles and they belong to groups which people like themselves join.

Staff, as the liveliest members of Mayfair, both in the affairs of the hotel and in the outside world, tend to have the highest status positions although people grumble about them all of the time. They are considered to be "the authorities" and their opinions about things are rarely challenged in public. They are seen by the residents as having two kinds of power -- power over their own lives and power over the residents. They decide who can come to live at the hotel and they can also decide to ask someone to leave. They have a monopoly over physical coercion because they can ask a resident to leave and they can also ask someone to go to his room if they feel he should be isolated from a social group. They are fully operative in the number 4 reality participation circle and the possession of the means of physical force bolsters their position even more. They themselves would probably deny this and declare themselves to be totally involved with "service to

8

the aged:. However, they are the ones who determine
what their service will be and who will benefit from
it and when.

The world of the hotel which is the total life
world to many residents is only the world of <u>work</u> to
the staff. They are involved in other worlds, in
other realities and are therefore often seen by residents as having a richer experience of life. This
makes their position here paradoxical. They are the
most active supporters of the life world at Mayfair--
the most ready to define the experience of life here.
Yet, the fact that they are not really <u>of</u> the life
world here makes them a subtle threat to the very
structure of experience they are trying to create
for the residents.

Nevertheless, the people who have the highest
status positions from the points of view of both
staff and residents are those who most resemble staff
in their actions and conversations. They are usually
active in number 3 or 4 reality participation circles
and they are likely to have a strong sense of responsibility about managing the place. They often come
to staff members and say: "I don't know what we are
going to do about such and such--". Lower status
residents tend to refer to staff and active residents
as "They" rather than "We". This terminology was
observed to occur among rebels, non-participant residents and senile residents. It expresses the sense
of not being a part of the life world whether from
exclusion or self-removal from it.

Background factors, health factors and deviations
of personality from what is considered to be a "good"
personality may cause an individual to be "left out"
socially and eventually seen to be in a low status
position from the point of view of the staff and other
residents. A person who is too well educated or
sophisticated may feel that the life world at Mayfair
is "small" and may choose to be separate from the
"lively" and "helpful" social groups. This person will
then be denied the status position in this community
which wisdom and experience should accord him or her.
A person who is too lively and pushes for more change
at the hotel than the staff wish to think about may be
pushed aside by them at meetings and acquire the reputation of being a person to whom no one listens.
Those who do not participate in the reality participa-
tion-social status structure as shown in Figure 1 are

not only those who are too senile to participate. They may be some of the most intellectually active residents who, out of cynicism refuse refuse to "play the game".

The Creation of Shared Meaning

There is another aspect of the life world of Mayfair House than the overt expression of social structure and reality participation circles. These aspects define the differences between residents. The world of shared meaning unites the residents and builds commonality. The residents are creating and interpreting their own cultural scene. Placing an individual in a reality participation circle and a status position on the basis of his conversation and actions tells us a great deal about the mechanics of social life. However, if we wish to understand what it is really like to live at Mayfair House it is necessary to try to determine through minute observation what are the concepts which residents share as a group. We then will see which ideas unite members of all reality participation circles and give the group whatever sense of community it has.

At Mayfair House there are differences in interpretation of everyday life based upon differences in past experience and in present reality participation circle. As we shall discuss more fully later, there is an "official view of Mayfair House imposed by the staff and management. In spite of differences there are large areas of shared meaning, centered mainly upon the life of the hotel and the interpretation of events here. The world outside the hotel is an area of dispute and one often hears residents arguing about what something they read in the newspaper "really meant". The group who sit in the card room have long discussions about why the President and (more often) the mayor did what they did. There is a large group of political conservatives who do a lot of talking about "the communists", but although most people agreed that the world was "worse than it used to be" there was no general consensus of opinion about the outside world.

The world of the hotel and its activities is the world of shared understanding and meaning. It is the sphere of everyday life, the face-to-face community. Inside the hotel the residents share experiences - three meals a day, social events and environment, both

10

physical and social, and leaders in the persons of
staff and the residents who help staff. There are
shared symbols which have evolved through time and the
social structure is endowed with certain meanings.
Events, such as the frequent breakdowns of the elevator
are given meaning in context of the total world of
the hotel.

To illustrate we shall give an example of meanings
and symbols which are shared by most of the residents.
To continue the subject of the elevators, the following conversation was recorded between four people
one morning:

Mr. Schwartz: It's no good, Harry. Don't try to
get up to your room. The elevator's not working
again and you'll never get the other one down
here.

Harry Green: Damn it! This is the second time this
week! The elevators are too old to repair and
Stone (the owner) is too cheap to get new ones.
He only runs this place to make money, doesn't
care about our inconvenience.

Mrs. Chittendon: You know, it doesn't matter how
much we complain. Nothing gets done to make the
elevators work well. You're right. They want our
money, but they don't care about our comfort!

Merle Johnson: Nothing makes you feel so helpless
as to have your room on the eighth floor with no
elevator working. I get so frustrated and angry.
It's true we're at the mercy of the corporation.
They don't care if we get mad and move out. They
will just get someone else in your room the next
day who doesn't know about the elevators. We just
don't matter.

Mr. Schwartz: Yeah, they give you a bill of goods
about how everything here is for your pleasure
and then you find out that you can talk forever
and not get any change in the things that need
changing.

The elevators are a bone of contention and the frequent
breakdowns are always interpreted to show: 1) the
indifference of the corporation to the people's
real needs, and 2) the relative powerlessness of the
residents in relation to the "bosses" - the corporation and staff. This is one of the most negative

shared meanings at Mayfair and it is voiced over and over in many different contexts. There is frequent turnover of staff, and once when a rather well-liked administrator was removed a woman said: "He was just too nice! Whenever they get a really good one who cares about us they take him out, because they want one who cares only about money." Not one person ever said that they thought that the hotel corporation was interested in anything but money. Even the resident leaders see their role as one of helping others to have a better life in relatively difficult conditions. The positive aspects of life at the hotel are considered to be the warm relations between some of the residents and the active social life. In opposition to these are the negative aspects of the indifference of the corporation and the domination of all areas of life by staff.

Just as the malfunctioning elevator is a symbol of the relative powerlessness of the residents, there are some more positive symbols recognized by all. Hilda Reilly, a resident of seven years has become the symbol of the "ideal retired person". She is a benevolent woman, active in charity and volunteer work who can always see the other person's point of view. She is well dressed, optimistic and present at all social events. When residents talk about good and useful people they almost always add -- "like Hilda Reilly". In all the time of the research no one said a bad word about Hilda, although other prominent residents received their share of criticism. Everyone seemed to approve of her, like her and respect her. When she stood up to speak in meetings everyone listened although they knew in advance the sort of thing she would say. Always cheerful, she says of herself that she likes to "accent the positive". She is a constant peacemaker and no one argues with her or is rude to her. Staff treat her with respect and often ask her opinion about matters pertaining to the hotel. To most of the residents she is the symbol of what a good retirement can be. Hilda thinks of herself as living now in her "golden years" and she lives this conviction so well that everyone else believes her. She is the symbol of the good things of old age. Her contentment is what all of the residents want for themselves and few have. Anyone who dislikes or attacks Hilda would be ostracized.

There is also a shared interpretation of the social hierarchy and the status positions in the hierarchy. It is understood that the high status positions belong to people who "do things". Power is thought to be concentrated in the staff and thus the people who associate most with staff and behave most like them are recognized as having a certain amount of power at the hotel. Everyone who was clear-headed enough to think about this, including rebels, agrees about status positions and power here. What they disagree about is how "good" or "bad" life is at the hotel and whether it is worthwhile to be involved in the activities here. A new resident who had been trying for some weeks to make a place for herself among the resident leaders knew that she had "arrived" when the social director asked her to take charge of a group outing. She said: "The social director asked me to take care of the group on Wednesday. It's kind of hard to manage, but she knows that I can keep them together and get everyone back on the bus at the right time." Acting as the leader of the group, she was able to use some of the power "lent" her by the staff to advance her own social standing in her drive to be an "Important Resident".

All residents agree that power is shown by associating with staff and being respected by them. All see the staff as the main authorities in the hotel community and the main source of power for residents. Staff then, as well as being at the top of the social hierarchy, are symbols of power in this group. They are admired and resented, watched and envied accordingly. One woman said of another: "She likes to act important, but have you noticed she never has any good ideas. The staff never listen to her even though she bothers them with her ideas all of the time

These and many other shared perceptions, interpretations, meanings and symbols give richness to the daily events of Mayfair House, surrounding everything that happens with a significance particular to this life world. Different reality participation circles are joined by a few threads of shared meaning giving areas of consensus to the extremely varied group of residents. Meaning emerges through continual comment and discussion of events, from the exchange of points of view between groups and from every alert residents' continual monitoring of the reactions of others. This process continually creates new areas of shared meaning and modifies the old ones so that in many ways the life at Mayfair House is anything but static

13

CHAPTER II

THE SHAPE OF LIFE AT MAYFAIR HOUSE

The 350 men and women who make their homes at Mayfair House are not prosperous. With perhaps one or two exceptions they are all just barely managing financially. Few of them have planned for old age and few have any substantial savings. Most of the residents have small pensions or Social Security checks each month but about 40% of them are on Public Aid. As we shall see, some of them have very little or no spending money left over after their rent (which includes meals) is paid. Rents vary at the hotel and are less for people on Public Aid. Money is a popular topic for discussion here, but residents do not like to have others know if they are on Public Aid, so there is some secrecy about checks. Because I was an outsider, people were quite willing to discuss their financial situations with me. What was important to them was that I promise not to tell any of the other residents anything about it.

Moving was not really possible for most of the residents. Many had had difficulty in finding a hotel like Mayfair, where the rent is reasonable; most had some relatives in the area; and many were just too timid to strike out again in a new location even if they had the opportunity. Some of the residents were behind in their rent payments and of course they could not move until they were paid up to date. There was a good deal of talk about moving, but the rate of turnover was very low. In fact, most of the people with whom one had contact had been at the hotel for over five years. The initial interviews with people always included the questions "How long have you been here?" and "Would you like to leave?" A few did want to leave and some did leave, but most of the people said that there were "problems" st Mayfair, but that they felt that they would rather stay. During the year of observation only two or three people left Mayfair House voluntarily. About ten to twelve people were asked to leave because of physical or mental health problems.

This varied group eats meals together in a communal dining room and they share five other public rooms and a patio. In the basement there are small rooms for crafts, billiards, meetings, and laundry. The hotel is old and well maintained except for the elevators whose erratic behavior is a great cause of anxiety and of strain in interpersonal relations.

The hotel has an old fashioned elegance which is striking as one enters. The lobby is red-carpeted with high ceilings and elaborate moldings, and dark wood reception desk faces the entrance. Chairs are totally absent from the scene (Figure 2). The lobby is the core of the building with all public rooms radiating from it. To the rear is the dining room. Approaching the dining room, two public rooms are visible, a theatre room on the left, and on the right a lounge with many chairs placed around the walls. The Social Director's office is an enclosed small room directly behind the reception desk. It has a feeling of being exactly in the center of the building. Except for a few minutes before the dining room doors are opened for meals, the lobby has few people in it other than several men who habitually stand there doing nothing. Standing about in the lobby is not encouraged, and since no chairs are provided, few people spend much of their time in this area. The atmosphere, except when the frequent quarrels over too-full elevators erupt, is peaceful and quiet. The reception desk is sometimes a conversation area with people chatting together or talking to the switchboard operator. Normally it is a relaxed and pleasant scene.

Upstairs there are several types of rooms available ranging from small ones with shared bath to quite large ones with private bath. Decoration in all of the rooms is austere and modern, although some of the residents manage to make their rooms charming and individual. Most of the rooms have no facilities for cooking or eating although some have a small stove and many residents keep small refrigerators for snacks and water heaters for coffee or tea during the day and evening.

The hotel is ten stories high and there are only three elevators, one a service elevator. Two are at the side of the main lobby and one is behind the dining room. As has been mentioned before, the elevators

Mayfair House Plan

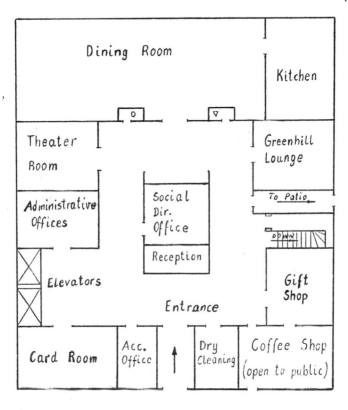

N

Dining Room

Kitchen

Theater Room

Greenhill Lounge

Administrative Offices

Social Dir. Office

To Patio

Reception

Elevators

Gift Shop

Entrance

Card Room

Acc. Office

Dry Cleaning

Coffee Shop (open to public)

Street

Figure 2

are temperamental. Thus, going upstairs and downstair
on the elevators' "bad days" becomes something of a
challenge. The unpredictability of the elevators
becomes one more vicissitude of life for the residents
People tend to try to limit their trips up and down
because they are unsure how long they will have to
wait for an elevator, or, and this is greatly feared,
that it will stop between floors and they will be
trapped.

The hotel is located in a deteriorated neighborhood which has many groups continuously involved in
neighborhood beautification and improvement efforts.[1]
An attractive new clinic and school very close to Mayfair House suggest that these efforts are succeeding
to a certain extent. However, there is danger for
old people here. Purse snatchings are common and
residents of Mayfair are counseled not to carry purses
or anything valuable when they go out. Several residents, during the time of this study, were injured
by being pushed to the ground by purse snatchers.
Although such a push might not have injured a younger
person, the results with the Mayfair residents were
broken bones, serious bruises, and nervous strain.

Ethnically the neighborhood is very mixed. White
of all nationalities, Blacks, Mexicans, Puerto Ricans,
and East Indians live there and can be seen on the
streets most of the time. To an outsider it is a
colorful and interesting area, made undesirable only
by the sense of constant danger. There are several
retirement facilities in the area and they are isolate
like ships at sea, loaded with quite vulnerable pas-
sengers. Among the Mayfair residents there is the
feeling that "outside" is unsafe and this tends to tur
people and their activities inwards to the hotel more
than they might have with a more welcoming outside
environment. The presence of a patio-garden in con-
junction with the hotel gives people a chance to be
out of doors without being exposed to the dangers
of the street. The garden is walled and it is for the
exclusive use of residents of the hotel.

In summertime all residents venture more outside
the hotel and garden. Women, particularly, usually
go out in pairs. Sometimes this is in order to help
each other to walk, but sometimes it is simply for
safety. The hotel is a kind of haven of safety in
a decidedly threatening environment. The other side
of the picture, however, is that the hotel is a kind

of prison in which people incarcerate themselves out of fear of the outside world. As in any institution which causes people to live in very close daily contact, there are many tensions and many techniques for dealing with these tensions. The social geography of Mayfair House is closely tied to the informal social life and to the social structure evolved in this community. Certain rooms and area are associated with certain groups and "types." Thus, there is a conceptual scheme accepted by most of the residents which divides not only "inside" and "outside" but subdivides "inside" into areas with definite social connotations. This will be further discussed in the chapter on informal social life.

Social life brings residents together. Often they withdraw from social life to relieve some of the pressures of overly close association. If people seem to be interacting too little, they are often resting from too much contact, too much interaction. Socializing is encouraged by the administrators and by most of the residents too, and it is thought of as a "good thing." However, many residents speak of the virtue of "not getting too involved" in the elaborate matrix of social life, gossip, and shifting allegiances.

Women appear to be much more active socially, but a few men are quite actively involved in social life--mainly in friendships with other men. Women at Mayfair socialize in more obvious ways, participating in committees, assisting in planned activities, and chatty behavior at the dining room tables. The effect is that the men seem much more passive and often, in fact, have less to do than the women. They appear to be "hanging around." Except for a few men who are extremely active, the men appear to the casual observer to be quite inactive. It is possible that their formal occupations were such that they did not develop techniques of looking busy when they were not, or of creating "busy work."

Coming from the outside world, the pace of life at Mayfair House seems very slow. Events do happen regularly and some days are exciting with crisis after crisis. Nevertheless, at first an observer feels that there is little to observe, that there is little happening. In fact, a great deal is happening all of the time. It is only after weeks of observation and quiet participation that the repeated patterns of social events, and the real social relationships become more clear.

It might be well to elaborate a bit upon the types of "non-events" and "non-conversations" which later turn out to have been real events and real conversations which were significant in the whole constellation of social events.

Example of a Seeming Non-Event

Mr. Rank is dressed to go out. He paces back and forth in front of the main entrance. He gives every evidence of waiting for someone. Mr. Boater walks by looking important and Mr. Rank addresses him. "I'm just waiting for my son to pick me up. You must have seen him. He's a big dealer in Cadillacs. He's driving a different one every time I see him." Mr. Boater completely ignores Mr. Rank. He neither looks at him nor replies.

As an isolated instance, one might suppose that either Mr. Boater is hard of hearing or dislikes Mr. Rank. Actually neither is true. Mr. Rank waits there for his son almost every day, and eight months of observation the sone was never seen to come and pick up his father. Therefore, most of the residents have come to take Mr. Rank's claims with a grain of salt, although some would stop to listen to him. Mr. Boater does not because he is one of the most important residents, one of the few men who are very busy. He probably did not stop to talk to Mr. Rank because he considered himself too busy to have to listen to the same story he had already heard so many times before. Most probably he had no ill will toward Mr. Rank at all. He simply discounted him as many adults discount or ignore a chattering child.

Example of a Seeming Non-Conversation

Mr. Schwartz and Mr. Smith meet in the hall. Mr. Schwartz is carrying a book. Mr. Smith says, "Hey, what is that book you have? Let me see." Mr. Schwartz shows him the book. It is a book about politics. Mr. Schwartz says "You're so nosy Smith." Mr. Smith replies, "Why do you always carry those books around with you when you never read them?" Mr. Schwartz says, "Get away from me Smith."

Mr. Schwartz and Mr. Smith are actually members of the same rather lively and thoughtful group of residents who like to keep themselves very distinct from less lively or "senile" people. A kind of teasing relationship is maintained and an interest in world affairs is assumed. After observing many conversations of this type it became clear that this was one of the means used to affirm membership in an "in-group" and to affirm one's role as a thinking as opposed to senile person.

Mr. Schwartz and Mr. Smith, in this seemingly nonsensical exchange are actually exchanging information about each other which is very important in maintaining their own roles and membership in a distinct social group. The joking, references to the book, and the casual way conversation is started and broken off are all elements which aid in identifying each other as members of that group and reaffirming their own membership.

Multiple patterns of meaning in the context of Mayfair House social life emerge after weeks and months of observation. None of the paterns is static, for change in groupings, roles, and "power" is always going one. To describe the pattern of social interaction for any one day or week is to describe something that has already undergone so many subtle changes that it may be metamorphasizing into something rather different even as it is being described.

Nevertheless, at any given time, it is possible to see the social life which is going on in terms of a set of distinct social groups, of a hierarchy of people and groups, and of leaders and "opinion formers" among the residents. Identification of the groups, hierarchy, and leaders gives an added dimension of meaning to the flow of group events which is constantly proceeding.

However, it is impossible to discuss social life at Mayfair House in reference to the residents alone, for the staff in such a retirement facility is of major importance.[2] In the rhetoric of the advertising brochures put out by Mayfair House, the staff is there to help the residents have an easier and fuller retired life. In the thinking of both staff and residents (expressed frequently in conversation), however the staff are the "bosses" and the residents must do as they are told. The staff are the top of the social pyramid, and are always the most noticed people at committee meetings, entertainments, and excursions. The stated philosophy of Mayfair House is one which en-courages active retirement, so any idea that staff are running things is discouraged. The following quote from a brochure makes this clear.

> When you live at Mayfair House you can't help but think active. Because all around you re-sidents are enjoying their retirement years with an enthusiasm that's hard to match. Good companions, an active social program, and people who care, make it easy to pick up the "Get Going" spirit.

> But even with all the opportunities at Mayfair, you're still as independent as you want to be, with your own apartment, friends and family.

Staff is simply not mentioned much in the advertising, but in this quotation, it is obvious that they are included in the category of "people who care." In conversation, the residents constantly refer to the staff as "the authorities" or "the bosses." Few are deceived as to the locus of power. One woman, an active leader, showed her awareness of the situation in a meeting. The meeting was concerned with main-tenance of the building. Many residents attended and there were numerous complaints about such matters as garbage in the halls, elevators which always break down, residents who go about in sloppy dress, cock-roaches in some of the rooms. The chairperson kept listening to all of the complaints and corroborations of complaints and repeating this statement time after time:

> Yes, that's a real problem. We must refer it to someone in authority. We can only hope that they will do something. I have no authority. I can only tell someone who does have authority.

It would be hard to count the number of times she af-firmed that she had no authority. If she and the other residents had felt that they were truly inde-pendent, her reply might have been:

> Yes, that's a real problem. I am going to ap-point a committee to go and discuss the matter with the administrator. We can't have condi-tions like that here.

In fact, no one spoke in this tone at the meeting. No

one disputed her rather passive approach to getting things done. There was general agreement that they must all <u>hope</u> for changes, and no suggestion that they must <u>insist</u> upon them.

The main staff personnel are the Administrator, Assistant Administrator, the Director of Food Services, and the Director of Social Planning. There are other staff, such as the Auditor, Chief Engineer, and two nurses, but the first mentioned four are of greater importance to the tenants because they have more contact with them, and their decisions affect all residents more directly.

During a year of observation at Mayfair House, only the Assistant Administrator and the Director of Food Services remained the same person. There were three Administrators and three Directors of Social Planning, and there was gossip that the third Administrator would be leaving soon (he did). Residents disliked, but expected constant change, and they learned to be philosophical about personnel whom they did not especially like because they felt that no staff member would be there very long.

The Administrator is the head of the whole Mayfair operation and he is directly responsible to the head of the corporation which owns Mayfair House. He is in constant communication with his superiors and is also frequently visited by a kind of roving Vice-President who goes to all of the corporations' hotels to "check up" on things. All matters concerning the hotel can be referred to him, although rentals are usually taken care of by the Assistant Administrator and matters of social significance such as dining room seating and entertainments are referred to the Director of Social Planning. He must decide when someone is too confused, too alcoholic, or too quarrelsome to continue as a resident of Mayfair House. He often must decide when someone is in need of care in a psychiatric facility, and he is the one who speaks to people who are long delinquent in paying their rent.

He holds weekly open meetings with the residents in which he informs them of any new developments at Mayfair. The residents are also asked to bring forward any questions or complaints they have during these sessions. Often quarrels break out among the residents at these meetings and the Administrator acts as peacemaker. He is addressed as "Mr. Tully" by most of the residents although he calls most of them by their first names.

The Assistant Administrator fills a similar role to the Administrator, although most residents feel more free to go to him with small matters. He often gives people a ride if they must go somewhere, and has done many personal favors for people. Although he is not always good humored, residents generally feel that they can count on him, and that he is "on their side." Except for being in charge of rentals, his functions are not too strictly defined and he is involved in many problems of the residents. He makes phone calls to Public Aid and Social Security, and often calls residents' families if they are ill or have some problem. He goes to residents' funerals and has often been the only one attending if the deceased had no family. Since he has been at Mayfair for about a year, residents consider him permanent.

The Director of Food Planning is a massive, pugnacious woman who has been at Mayfair for over eight years. She is given to displays of temper and her long years of work at Mayfair make the rest of the staff more ready to tolerate them than if she had come more recently. She is the only staff member ever seen to have made constant open displays of her superior power. She holds weekly sessions of a Dining Room Committee during which residents are supposed to give their ideas, criticisms, and compliments regarding the food. In these sessions she sits at a long table in the front of the Theatre Room along with the president of the committee (a resident) and the secretary who calls on the members of the committee one by one, asking them if they have "anything to say." Criticisms are usually met with excuses and explanations, or with an occasional admission of a mistake. Her position is that she knows food and knows prices and that her role is to explain to residents why they were served something they did not like. A question about why pork was never served was countered by a lecture on why pork is not good for older people. Many questions about why something is not served are answered with a "we can't afford it."

This committee is frustrating to many residents because they have observed that however much they talk or ask for certain changes, the changes are never made. As a result many of the people who attend are there

23

to tell "Mrs. Food Services" how much they liked this
or that meal. A group of very pleasant ladies can be
counted upon to soften any criticism of the food or
service with dozens of compliments on the taste of
the food, the look of the food, the service, the place-
mats, etc. Many dissatisfied residents become disgusted with this performance and never come to the
Dining Room Committee Meetings. There is a certain
amount of fear in the residents' relations with the
Food Service Director. Food is important to everyone,
and perhaps more important to older people who are
quite set in their tastes. The Food Service Director
never lets people forget that she can withhold things
that people really like--such as ice cream and water-
melon--if they are too loud in complaining about the
things they don't like--such as raw liver and tough
spaghetti. As long as residents are humble and re-
spectful, she is benevolent, but the least display of
anger or aggressiveness bring out double the anger and
aggressiveness from her. Her state of health is precarious as she suffers from serious stomach ulcers
and she often mentions this to residents. She was
hospitalized twice in eight months.

Three women have occupied the position of Director
of Social Planning during the last year. It is a
position which requires contact with the residents,
and a great deal of planning of their activities. The
Social Director must put out the printed schedule of
weekly events and she is also an informal editor of
the monthly newsletter put out by the residents. She
arranges seating in the dining room, makes announcements of daily events in the dining room, arranges,
and often goes along on excursions. She introduces
speakers and celebrity guests and is also required to
try to enforce the Mayfair dress code. All of the
three social directors were apparently very busy and
were in constant motion about the building. Many of
the residents felt that they should not bother the
social director with their problems because "she has
so much to do." The first social director during the
research period was a cordial person. She always
apologized for not having time, but she would never
engage in an extended conversation with anyone. She
was always just in the midst of some work which had
a deadline, or just about to leave for somewhere else.
However, she did allow residents to sit in her office
all day long, and she kept a television set turned
on so that they could sit there and watch it. Her
office became a kind of club with a few "regulars" who

were always sitting there, simply watching everything which went on. The presence of a number of residents in her office also acted as a deterrent to any serious discussion with any one resident. The office was "cleared" only when the social director wanted to talk with some staff or a visitor came with some sort of confidential matter.

A change of policy which was a major social upheaval for some of the residents occurred when the second Social Director arrived. Being apparently unwilling to work in a fishbowl atmosphere, she declared the Social Director's office to be out of bounds except when a resident had a particular problem or errand to carry out there. No one was to sit there watching the scene hour after hour. The former "regulars" were angry, hurt, and even rather disoriented, because they had lost the focus of a major part of their day. There was a great deal of complaining, some expressions of anger, and talk of "the place didn't used to be so unfriendly." The worst thing was to see those who had spent much of their day in the office casting aimlessly about for another location. One man in particular seemed to cut back drastically on his social life. He was not often seen in the public rooms or even in the hall. He appeared only for special events and entertainments From being very much in the center of things, he became much more peripheral. In the days when he had been able to sit in the Social Director's office he often said: "I'm never in my room. I come down in the morning and come in here (the office), and I don't go back up until it's time for bed." He had been very proud of being active and involved. At the time the research ended, he had still not established an equally involved pattern for himself because he had no location where he could be a part of what was going on.

The third Social Director came at the end of the research period and had not fully established her policy when the observation stopped. It appeared, however, that she would not be as strict in preserving her office as a strict business area. A few people had already begun to sit there for rather extended periods of time. If the residents have their way, her office will soon become a club or meeting center again. From the point of view of creating a happy living experience for the residents, this would be a good thing. There was no other "staff area" where the residents could meet informally with staff without having a particular matter to discuss. Without this type of meeting ground, the gulf between staff and residents is far too wide. Combined with the sense that the residents have that the staff is terribly busy, they can feel neglected without some type of informal contact. Just a smile from the Social Director and the chance to sit in her office for a time and see what she is doing gives some residents a feeling that they have an idea of what is going on, and a sense of participation in the hotel in all its activities.

The residents are very dependent upon these four key staff members, and the unfortunate thing is that there are so many residents for so few staff. There are other people who figure in the life of the residents. There is the auditor, the receptionist-switchboard operation, and staff aides (like myself during the research), all of whom are called upon for a variety of matters. A resident may discuss his family problems with the receptionists, ask the auditor to direct him to a certain store, or ask an aide to find him a funeral director for his future funeral. In one case it was the auditor who noticed that one of the residents had been missing for several days, and began the process of location him. Even the janitors and maids are often doing things other than their regular jobs--in connection with needs of the residents. This, and the fact that the staff is often too busy to handle any but the most crucial problems points out the need for more "helpers" if not more staff.

Mayfair House is a very busy place with much activity. Social life for the elderly residents here may appear to proceed at a leisurely pace, but for those who participate, it is quite intense. The staff is the hub and the initiator of most of the activity of a planned sort, but informal social life also takes place in a very lively way. As we will discuss in later chapters, there are people who do not take part in social life, but they still affect the social life of the more gregarious residents-mainly as negative examples of how one should not live.

Bearing in mind the image of Mayfair House as a large hotel with many residents, few staff, and some complex social problems, we can proceed to a more detailed examination of social life. First and foremost in Mayfair House advertising is the description of their lively planned social program. Therefore, we shall begin with a discussion of the planned social program, and proceed to capture the details of the informal social life later.

Footnotes to Chapter II

1. There was evidence that the neighborhood was developing facilities especially geared to the large population. Officers from nearby banks came to tell residents of their services, and there were convenient pharmacies and small shops. Harlan (1954) describes community adaption to a large elderly population in St. Petersburg, Florida. More conveniences for the elderly were envisioned as part of neighborhood improvement plan in the Mayfair area.

2. Here again, Kleemeier's (1954) discussion of the problem of staff directing too much of the social life is pertinent. Staff were very obvious at Mayfair. At one time their special table in the dining room was in the center near the door so it was the first thing one saw upon entering. There was a large sign on it which said "Staff."

CHAPTER III

PLANNED SOCIAL LIFE

In the advertising brochures, the planned social life of Mayfair House is given primary coverage. It stresses a lively retirement, free of lonliness, and suggests, less openly, that the staff of Mayfair House will free one from the problem of trying to think of things to do. The brochures paint a glowing picture of activities, excursions, crafts, meetings and social involvement in the community. The social program is geared to getting people to do things which they might not have done if they had had to organize them themselves. A sample program of events in an advertising circular listed all of these activities as a "typical" week:

Monday: Fascinating Mah Jongg, mosaic tile or
            ceramics class, art class for beginners,
            foreign language class for beginners,
            slimnastics.

Tuesday: Choral group with "sing-along", Folk
            dance lessons, Music appreciation class.

Wednesday: Sewing classes, stamp club meetings,
            and bridge classes.

Thursday: Canasta, bridge, mah jongg, sketching,
            and social dancing.

Friday: Group meetings for civic discussion,
            music appreciation, garden walks.

Saturday: Sightseeing walks on lakefront, fishing
            in Lake Michigan.

Sunday: Special Chapel services, special Sunday
            dinner, occasional bus trips to museums,
            Sunday evening entertainment.

Some of these activities such as "garden walks" or "fishing in Lake Michigan" were obviously meant to be done on individual initiative, but it is the policy at Mayfair to have special planned activities for groups of residents each day. A substitute Social Director who came in while the regular one was on vacation said: "It's terribly hard. I have to have something special for every day!" The actual daily programs are not as full as the advertising suggests, but there is usually some special event each day-- a speaker, musical entertainment, or a special class.

The purpose of all of the planned activities is to get people together and to keep them busy. The staff does not want residents to sit in their rooms alone, or to vegetate either alone or in groups. The idea is to get them involved and to keep them involved and active. Mayfair House requires that residents be in fairly good health to be accepted, although this qualification applies more to physical than to mental health. Formerly a physician's report was required, but this was no longer the case. Again and again one hears "This is not a nursing home. It is a residential hotel for people who can take care of themselves." This is said by both staff and residents. Being able to take care of oneself, however, is not simply a matter of being able to walk to the dining room three times a day and to dress oneself. It is a total state of capability which many of the residents in no way achieve. Those who are indeed capable are often very resentful that others who are less capable, give the place a "nursing home atmosphere," and often cause great concern. The fact that all residents are supposed to be healthy means that no special services such as giving out of medicines, or checking whether everyone has appeared for meals, are provided. It is up to the residents to help each other out in these ways. This they are willing to do to a certain extent, but rightfully they become worried if they feel that they have too much responsibility for someone who is really incompetent.

The activities, then, are planned for the physically and mentally active residents, although there is some pretense that they are for everyone. Entertainments, committees and meetings, excursions, and parties are the most important activities. There is variety in the activities and it is expected that there will be something for every interest. Staff and residents disapprove if an individual does not

participate in any of the activities. It is considered
unfriendly and the person who isolates himself from
all of the events is looked upon with suspicion.

In fact, there were few residents who would not at
least listen to a musical group if one were performing in the theatre. Even the most isolated individuals would wander in to listen to a speaker for a
few minutes and then, perhaps, wander out again. In
every activity there were three types of participation
(1) Full participation; (2) half participation; and
(3) peripheral participation. In any event, those who
were fully participating would sit at the front of
the room, or in a conspicuous place, and would engage
with what was happening either by conversation or by
fairly intense eye contact. Those who were half
participating would sit at the back or in incon-
spicuous positions and would not speak, occasionally
lapsing into their own thoughts. Those who were
peripheral participants would never be fully involved
with the event. They would wander in and out, fall
asleep, or try to talk to others about something other
than what was happening. The peripheral participants
were often very much resented by the others because
of the disturbances they caused. One lady never
failed to appear for speakers, but she would leave
after about five minutes, and then return and leave
again as many as six times. She was extremely irritating to a number of residents who would respond
to all this with shouts of "Sit down!" "Come in or
stay out!" Another peripheral participant who had
come into a musical performance and wanted to "sing
along" when this was not part of the program aroused
a rush of anger, resentment, and fear that the en-
tertainer from outside would "think we are all as
crazy as she is." This occasion also relates to the
problem of creating a good public image of Mayfair
House which will be discussed at length later.

It would be hard to determine, considering the
disapproval heaped upon the peripheral participants,
whether staff and residents would prefer peripheral
participation or no participation at all. However,
when a guest speaker was coming, the Social Director
seemed more concerned with filling the theatre with
an audience than with anything else. Often she
could be seen standing by the dining room door after
lunch urging people to come in, in this fashion.
"Come in and sit down. You won't want to miss this
show. It's going to be beautiful! You absolutely

must see it. You'll love it! Come in!" If the
guest were very prominent, there was more pressure
to "fill the house," and residents would be practi-
cally herded to the theatre.

Although, upon such occasions, numbers of people
present were of importance, and, in the rhetoric of
Mayfair advertising every one should participate,
both staff and residents were aware that the actual
situation was a bit different. A very small number
of residents actually were full participants in any
of the planned activities. Moreover, in every
activity, it was usually the same people who were
active. The staff was very grateful for this small
core, and tended to depend upon them for support and
for giving a good impression to guest on all occasions.
This small group is actually living the retirement
philosophy of Mayfair House, proving that it is not
an impossibility or a fantasy. It is for this
small group of people that all of the activities
program is really planned. They, in their interest
and lively participation, exemplify the approved
attitude. They are the ones who speak for Mayfair
House. One of the residents, present at a discussion
group, wrote a letter to the editor of a local newspaper which went somewhat as follows:

No One Knows about Retirement Hotels

There seems to be much misunderstanding about
what a retirement hotel is. I am a senior citizen
who has appeared on the radio to clear up mis-
conceptions....First, a retirement hotel is not a
shelter care facility or a nursing home. It caters
to people who are totally capable of taking care
of themselves.....The cultural and recreational
program covers a broad spectrum of activities and
events. Speakers from many areas of interest
are brought in for weekly discussion programs.
We have weekly entertainment, both profes-
sional and community, and hobby classes with tal-
ented instructors....Although the retirement
hotel is primarily a residence for senior citizens,
we are not cut off from the rest of the community.
We are able-bodied men and women who go with freedom and frequency to cultural and social events
around the city. We visit friends and have guests
visiting us.
....If there were more places like Mayfair House
there would be fewer senior citizens living

along and angry with the world.

Mary Hammersmith, President
World Today Discussion Group

Mrs. Hammersmith's attitude represents completely
the ideas about life and Mayfair House which the
staff would like to see in all residents. The project
is always to get more residents of this type, and less
of the more passive and less capable type.1

It might be well to consider in a more detailed way
what actually takes place in the various categories
of activities. The most highly attended type of
activity is the entertainment. If a celebrity is
coming, many residents will make a special effort to
be present.

One day in winter a great stir went around all of
the Mayfair public rooms. A vice president of the
corporation had arrived to inform the Administrator
that Mayfair could expect a visit from a very famous
person that afternoon. The visitor was to be an
actress known to all of the residents for her beauty,
multiple marriages, and extravagant life style. She
is also a frequent guest on popular talk shows, so
her personality was extremely familiar. Most of the
residents just wanted to "see if she really looks that
good up close." The staff was worried that she might
simply walk out if something didn't just suit her.
They were worried about her famous temperament if
she did arrive, and worried about terrible loss of
face with the residents if she did not arrive.

A reception was arranged with an elaborate chocolate cake. Staff then began to worry about what she
was actually going to do as entertainment. They got
the word that she would not give a proper talk, but
would answer resident's questions about her life,
opinions, etc. The aspect of this which frightened
the staff was the possibility that the residents
would be so overwhelmed that they would not be able
to think of any questions--a distinct possibility.
They tried to solve this by writing a number of questions on slips of paper and giving them to some of
the more active residents, asking them to "help"
by asking them. Finally, the hall was full of rather
bemused residents, some holding white cards, no one
knowing just when the famous guest would arrive.

As it happened, she arrived while the second seating at lunch was being served--a nightmare to the Social Director who begged them to leave their tables and go to the theatre, promising that lunch would be saved for them. A few residents got up and went to the theatre, but the majority insisted upon finishing their lunch, although they ate a bit more quickly than usual.

In the meantime, the famous guest was threatening to leave if an audience were not assembled at once. She was accompanied by a manager, who forwarded her complaints to the staff, and by a patient small dog wearing a blue ribbon. At last, before all was lost, the audience was summarily assembled and the event could take place. A resident began playing romantic tunes on an ancient piano and the <u>Star</u> walked down the aisle. She was given a Star's introduction by the Social Director, and began a charming greeting to the residents. She complimented them on their hotel and then offered to answer any questions that they had. After a short pause, the reliable residents with the question slips began to ask questions. She replied to them all amusingly and everyone laughed appreciatively. There were not enough questions, so the administrator and the Social Director began to ask everything they could think of. A small boy who happened to be there asked "What is your favorite kind of fur?" and everyone laughed. The Star replied: "I don't really like fur at all!--I only wear it to make other girls jealous!" More laughter and then it was time to close and go to the reception. The residents who had asked the questions were heroes-- first because they had talked to the Star and secondly, because they had helped to make the entertainment succeed. The romantic music was begun again and the Star tried to make her exit. It was a rather unsuccessful exit because her way was blocked by a number of residents who had started to leave first and were filling the aisles. Somehow she was extricated from the traffic jam by the Social Director, and was escorted to a lounge to shake hands with many of the resients, to have her picture taken with them, and to have the first piece of cake.

Residents crowded to the reception--perhaps more for the cake than for the Star, but a lively atmosphere was created. Pictures were taken and many residents exchanged a word or two with the famous guest. After a short time she took her leave, and suddenly staff and residents realized how exhausted they were. It had been a major production for them, and it was unclear who was entertaining whom. Nevertheless, the quick glimpse of the life of the famous was exhilarating, though exhausting for the residents who had participated. The temperament of the star and her lack of a set sort of entertainment had forced staff and residents to cooperate to make the event a success. The staff wanted the event to be successful, and the residents who helped were concerned with not letting down their staff or Mayfair House.

Most entertainments are simply spectator events and in the time of the research there was not another occasion on which both staff and residents worked so hard and so cooperatively. Both were equally concerned that the event proceed successfully, and therefore coordinated their efforts to an unusual extent. However, with every guest, residents are well aware of the image they are expected to project, and most try to cooperate, and to be happy and alert retired people.

Meetings and committees which are part of the planned activities program take up the largest amount of time at Mayfair House. There is a Dining Room Committee, a House Maintenance Committee, a Volunteer Aid Committee, and there was a Current Events Discussion Group which was almost inactive at the time of research. In addition, there are small committees which organize religious services for each faith and a committee which gives a tea for new residents periodically. It is not surprising after spending time at Mayfair House, that each committee is composed of nearly the same people, and the same people attend each of the meetings regularly. There are about forty people at Mayfair who can be expected to be at meetings and to play a full or partial participant role. These people seem to feel involved with what is going on and to feel that they are taking part in policy-making, even though some become cynical about the results of all their discussion. As has been discussed before, many of the really active participators were no longer coming to the Dining Room Committee meetings because they felt that they and their ideas were being completely ignored by the Food Director.

A more successful committee is the House Maintenance Committee. Like all of the committees it has a staff sponsor who is there to take note of what the residents are saying, and to take action if necessary.

The staff sponsor usually sits at the front of the room at a long table with the Chairman, Vice-Chairman, and Secretary of the committee. Typically, the meeting is opened by the Chairman, and after time for corrections of the minutes, the group is asked to present any new business. A typical dialogue at a House Maintenance Committee meeting would be as follows:

Chairman: "No one has any corrections of the minutes, so we can move on to new business now. First of all, I'd like to say that you don't have to wait until you have a complaint to say something. You can always say something is nice."

Mrs. A.: "Well, I'd like to be able to say something nice, but I'm very upset about the trash on the eighth floor. People are not putting their trash into the containers. They are just putting it out into the hall and the smell is awful, and cockroaches are coming."

Mrs. B.: "That's true on the second floor too, and I have told people I've seen leaving their trash in the hall, but they just get mad at me and tell me to mind my business and shut up."

Mrs. C.: "There's a man on our floor who puts his beer bottles outside his door. Someone told him to put them into the trash chute, and he said he would, but he just forgets no matter how many times he is told."

Mr. D.: "The trouble is there are too many people here who just can't remember. Everyone here is supposed to be able to take care of himself."

Mrs. A.: "It wasn't that way six years ago when I moved in here. The people were a better group. Now they'll take anyone who's alive."

Staff Sponsor: "Everyone here is supposed to be able to take care of himself and participate in the life here. We try to be careful who is admitted. Mr. Tully is constantly reviewing the situation."

Mr. D.:   "Yeah. We all know that this corporation is
            in business to make money and that they
            want the rooms here full."

Chairman: "Just a minute, we're getting away from the
            subject. We should all be responsible for
            the condition of the halls on our floors.
            If we see someone littering, we should
            tell him nicely where the waste chute is,
            and if he forgets we should keep on re-
            minding him. I agree that we shouldn't
            have to, but if we don't want cockroaches
            we will all have to watch for litter and
            litterers."

Staff
Sponsor: "I will ask George and his crew to go up to
            the halls more often and look for litter,
            but if everyone would just take care of his
            own litter it would be so much nicer for
            you all."

Mrs. B.:   "It makes me so angry when I see trash in the
            hall. This is my home and I don't want to
            live in a dump! People who mess up the
            halls should be asked to leave."

Mrs. A.:   "They really should not let just everyone
            come and live here. I wonder if they kept
            their own houses that way when they had
            them."

Chairman: "We'll all have to be more careful--Now
            let's move on to something else........

This conversation was repeated in slightly different
forms many times over in House Maintenance Committee
meetings. There was a constant struggle between residents who wanted the hotel to be in good condition
and clean, and those who simply did not care, or who
forgot to take care of things such as garbage. There
was constant frustration on the part of those who did
care, and a feeling that the staff should be doing
more to help them out. The frequent meetings, however
did serve to remind staff of the serious problem of
different orientations and capability levels among
the residents.

    Meetings are open to everyone, and so there are
usually a number of people who wander in and out and
many who sit at the back and sleep. Those who never

37

participate seem to come because the meeting gives them somewhere to go, even if they only listen or go to sleep. The active members complain about those who go to sleep, or chat to each other in the back of the room, but they are even more irritated if people don't come to the meetings at all. One House Maintenance Committee was adjourned when only ten or eleven people came, and those few had nothing special to discuss. The chairman was completely disgusted, complaining that there was so much to be done and no one willing to try to help make it get done. Active residents have little tolerance of the inactive and uninvolved ones. They feel that they are doing a great deal of work for these people with no help from them and no appreciation either. Appreciation of the active members comes from each other and from the staff who realize that a few residents act as unpaid staff members--checking up on things in the building and reporting things which should be repaired.

Active members of the Volunteer Aid Group are especially helpful--doing things which none of the staff have time to do, such as escorting people to the clinic, downtown for shopping, or shopping for others who are ill or feel unable to go out. The Volunteers also visit any residents who have gone to the hospital, and see that they receive a card. The Volunteer Group gives a number of awards, such as gold and silver pins, volunteer of the month, volunteer of the year, etc.--which members can earn if they draw the attention of the group by outstanding service. This group is slightly different from the other committees, because, in spite of the fact of the awards for service, their attitude is that they ought to be helping each other. They are more tolerant of incompetent residents, although some have said privately and in meetings that taking care of some of the really confused or immobile residents has at times become a risk to their own health. One outstanding volunteer, a tall immaculate white-haired woman who has herself suffered three strokes, complained privately that she was in extreme distress because she was helping so many people that her blood pressure had become dangerously high. Her doctor, she said, had told her to "take it easy" and to spend part of each day resting. Because she was known as an active volunteer, people were calling upon her for help day and night. She said she was really unable to refuse them. Thus, her health was deteriorating and she was extremely nervous. She wanted to be active but felt unable to be as active as she was being at the time.[2]

This case points to the important fact that the facility is very understaffed.[3] There should be staff members with enough time to take on some of the burdens of the volunteers.

Parties are a very popular form of social life at Mayfair. Residents who do not come to the entertainments, speakers, and meetings will often show up for a party. Every month there is a birthday party for all of the residents who have had birthdays that month. This consists of a special dinner, with all the birthday people seated at one table. There is a special dinner, and of course, there is also a big cake, and everyone sings "Happy Birthday." The following is a quote from the residents' newsletter about the July 1975 birthday party:

> Nineteen Mayfair House Residents celebrated the Bicentennial year of the United States because their birthdays were in July 1975. They attended a happy dinner at the staff table in the Kensington Dining Room. They were served cantaloupe, fried chicken, baked potatoes, peas and a cherry chocolate whipped cream layer cake by our nice waiters....Mrs. Thomasina Treadwell, one of the birthday celebrants played several songs on the piano and there was loud clapping by the other residents as they sang "Happy Birthday.".....Those who celebrated their birthdays represent 1,341 years of living. They came from all nationalities and when they were younger they were in business and professional lines. There were celebrants who were doctors, dentists, lawyers, nurses and teachers......A Happy Birthday to all those July birthday babies!

by The Editor

There is a welcome party given for new residents. At this party the newcomers are introduced, asked to tell their life stories, and are served tea, coffee, and pastries. At first, this party was open to all residents, but later it was restricted to the newcomers and the Welcoming committee. It seems that a of the residents had come before in such numbers for the drinks and pastries, that they were always running out of refreshments—often before the new people had had any. Therefore, this party is now a smaller one with restricted attendance. Everyone who mentioned this fact felt that it was unfair.

One rather successful party which took place during the research was a 59th wedding anniversary celebration for a couple living at Mayfair. The staff went to a good deal of trouble for this occasion. All of the furniture in the dining room was moved to create an area for a receiving line and regular wedding reception. A huge and beautiful cake with the numbers 59 in gold on the top had been bought for the guests. The Food Director said that the cake was from the best bakery in the city and that it had cost about $80.00. There was great excitement among the residents--mostly concerning the cake which they had heard about. The reception was held at about three o'clock in the afternoon and almost everyone at Mayfair House was there to hear the music and to congratulate the anniversary couple. The only problem was that, although it was huge the cake was not quite huge enough. Some of the residents received no cake, or only a tiny piece. Some of the residents who had had to be elsewhere and had asked their friends to save them a piece of cake were chagrined to find that they had none upon their return.

Seemingly unimportant problems like getting no cake are often very significant at Mayfair. As soon as it became obvious that there was to be a shortage of cake, some of the residents began to accuse each other of "taking the biggest piece," "taking two pieces," "pushing ahead in line," and other unpleasant things. To a certain extent some of the residents forgot the purpose of the party, which was to offer congratulations to the celebrating couple, and became involved in serious arguments about the cake. The importance of the "treat" at any party cannot be minimized.

Another instance of quarrels over food occurred when one of the Mayfair classes, taught by a college teacher from a nearby community college decided to turn its last meeting into a party. They selected a gift for the teacher, and a committee ordered chocolate eclairs from the kitchen. After a short concluding class, the group went into one of the public lounges to have refreshments and to present the gift. As soon as the refreshments appeared, other residents who had not been members of the class began to come in--expecting to eat. A member of the party committee began turning them away, saying "This is a private party just for members of the Psychology class." Instead of retreating, some of the residents began to fight. One woman began to cry saying: "I can see that you have chocolate eclairs. They are my favorite. I just felt like a chocolate eclair. You can't keep me out. You're so mean!" Before it was settled, quite a scene ensued with some of the residents determined to gate-crash and the committee determined to keep them out. For many days the incident was discussed and was a source of bad feeling between members of the class and those who had been excluded from the refreshments. There was some feeling that if any refreshments were served at Mayfair they should be for everyone, as it is everyone's "home." It was also argued that there would be less cake parties if each one had to serve enough for 350 people. There was also discussion of people who never came to events to participate, but only came to eat afterward, often taking more than their fair share. Altogether, the feeling emerged that the active people, as a group, were "carrying" too many inactive people whom they saw as parasites. They felt that those who contributed nothing to a class or committee had no right to come clamoring for refreshments. There was a great deal of bitterness in this feeling, and many of the active people expressed extreme disillusionment with the quality of life at Mayfair.

Earlier in the chapter three types of participation in the planned social life were delineated: (1) Full participation; (2) half participation; and (3) peripheral participation. Now it might be well to consider who is to be found in each of these categories. Months of observation led to the inescapable conclusion that, although numbers of men and women at Mayfair are approximately the same, more women participate in all types of planned social activity than men. Men tended to come to movies and speakers more than to other activities, but they were always outnumbered. In the committees, men were conspicuous by their absence or by their presence in very small numbers. A count kept to attendance at two committees during the spring and summer of 1975 shows attendance as follows:

House Maintenance Committee

April   --   16 women
             3 men

May   --   10 women
             1 man

June   -   34 women
                     6 men

July   -   meeting called off because
                only about 10 women came

August   -   45 women
                  4 men

Dining Room Committee

March   -   65 women
                  11 men

April   -   Meeting 1
                   42 women
                    4 men

                   Meeting 2
                   38 women
                    2 men

May   -   38 women
                   4 men

June   -   29 women
                   0 men

July   -   33 women
                   1 man

August   -   42 women
                  1 man

September -35 women
                  0 men

In the colder months attendance by both men and women at committees is better, but the proportions remain about the same. Disucssions with the Social Directors and Administrators always gave the same answer--the women are more active in the planned social life than the men, and strikingly so. The staff say that this has been their experience at other retirement facilities as well. Also, more men than women at Mayfair can be observed standing or sitting about doing nothing.

As was mentioned in Chapter I, a number of seemingly confused men **stand in the lobby** at Mayfair doing what appears to be absolutely nothing but staring. They make no pretence of being about to go somewhere or of waiting for someone, but simply stand there, often for long periods of time. This habit cannot be attributed to confusion alone, for there are as many equally confused women who cannot be found standing in the lobby. Rather, it may be suggested that the roles which these men and women were accustomed to playing in their lives before retirement, fitted the women better for making the small tasks of the day fill the day, and for making them appear occupied when they actually have nothing in particular to do. It is interesting to note that the men whom we shall later discuss as leaders make a great point of stressing how busy they are, and are never observed to stand still doing nothing.

Therefore, with a few exceptions, the active participants in the planned social life of Mayfair are women. Age has little to do with active participation, but mental alertness is very important. For example, the ages of the principal officers of the main committees are as follows: House Maintenance Committee--President, a woman 62, Vice-President, a woman 70, Secretary, a woman 73; Dining Room Committee--President, a woman 83, Vice-President, a woman 72, Secretary, a woman 59; Volunteer Society--President, a man 85, Vice-President, a man 70, Secretary, a woman 59. One of the discussion groups was led by an 84 year-old woman; a writing group was formed by a 62 year-old woman; and an exercise class was held by a 74 year-old woman. Age is an important topic of discussion at Mayfair, but it is not the most important factor in determining how active an individual will be socially.

Naturally, general health is a significant factor, and all who could be called leaders in any sense present a picture of a certain amount of vigor. However, although they seem energetic, many of the active participants in all events are physically frail, and many of the most inactive are physically robust. Mental sharpness and a desire to participate are the significant factors. This is one of the difficulties faced by the staff when they are deciding whether to accept an individual as a resident at Mayfair. Often people with good health records who seem very capable cannot be counted upon to parti cipate in the life of Mayfair and make social events successful.

About 25-30 people at Mayfair can honestly be said to be full participants in the planned activities. Perhaps 125-150 are half participants in a large part of the activities. The remaining 100 or more are only peripheral participants. The ideals of the social planning suggest that everyone should be a full participant, therefore, it is easy to see that the planned social events often have a cumbersome feeling--having such a minimum full participation. The active residents, as has been pointed out, feel that too much social responsibility rests upon them. One hears remarks such as: "We're all retired here, and we should all be looking after our health, but some people just want to sit back and let everyone else do the work. They just want to come to all the parties and eat, but they don't want to help." Many times the remark was heard that: "There are too many selfish people here. They can't get along with any-one. Probably they couldn't get along with their families and that's why they're here." All the people with whom long conversations were held, ex-pressed disillusion with the types of people they had encountered at Mayfair. All who expressed this feeling added that they had "not known that there were people like that, so mean and selfish!" A few attributed the difficulties they had with other re-sidents to old age and the fact that some people "get very strange when they get old." A larger percentage complained about "the class of people they let in here." A number of long-time residents said that there had formerly been, " a nicer group of people." When pressed to explain further, most would say: "Many of the people here are uneducated. They don't know how to behave." One articulate Jewish man, Mr. Fish, said: "I don't know about Gentiles here, but I do know about the Jews. Jews are not all alike, there are classes and levels. I come from a good family, and I know that the Jews here are of the lowest type. I really don't know where they found these people. They know absolutely nothing. I have tried, but there is nothing that I can talk about with them."

Not all of the people who expressed dismay with their fellow residents were active participants in social life. Although the active people did express a great deal of disillusion about their fellow re-sidents, the half and peripheral participants also

expressed the same disillusion, and often stated
that they did not "get involved in things" because
"people were too difficult" or "no one appreciates
anything you do." Many of the half participants
had formerly played a more active part, but had withdrawn a bit from activities because they had become
discouraged. A very few residents actively avoided
any participation in any of the planned activities
as an expression of their disillusion with their
fellow residents.

Therefore, among the residents who never participate in the activities, we can distinguish two
groups: (1) those who are staying away to avoid contac
with other residents, and (2) those who are not mentally acute enough to remember that something is
planned, or who are simply living too completely in
their own worlds to be aware of much in the way of
external activities. Most of the residents participate some of the time in a sort of half participant
role. Almost all of the residents are brought into
some of the activities, whether they planned on it or
not. Birthday parties and special events centering
around the dining room (for example, "Italian Night")
include respectively everyone who has had a birthday that month and everyone who is in the dining
room.

The planned activities program does bring people
together and for those that wish, it gives a skeleton
of meetings and events around which to plan their
day. What it does not seem to do for most residents
is to reproduce the feeling of an active social life
in the world "outside." This, it seems, is partly
because of the contingent of peripheral participants
who hover around the fringes of each event--not
really there, and yet there. Their partial presence
throws a question upon the reality of any event, and
make the planned activities hard to sustain at times.
Goffman (1963: 75-79) discusses this problem under
the rather obscure sounding category of "Occult
involvement." He uses this term to describe the
disturbing effect of people who are not really
involved in an activity upon those who are involved
in it. [4] He states that the feeling that the person
is there and yet not really there is most disconcerting: "Perhaps it is this quality of not being
present and not being readily recallable to the
gathering, rather than the specifics of the impro-
per conduct itself, that creates the disturbing

impressions" (1963:77). The large numbers of peripheral participants in every event at Mayfair does create a disturbing atmosphere for those who wish their social life at the hotel to have the same sense of normalcy and mutually accepted reality which they had experienced in their social life before retirement. They consider themselves to be trying to experience social life on their terms in the face of tremendous difficulty from other residents who unintentionally thwart them at every turn.

Footnotes to Chapter III

1. "Disengagement" as articulated by Cumming and Henry (1962) was not accepted in the Mayfair "philosophy" as part of the normal aging process. Activity was stated as both the norm and the ideal even though not all of the residents were active.

2. No matter how active an elderly person is there are times when he or she wants to rest. Simmons states desire for rest as a universal of aging in Aging in Preindustrial Society, Handbook of Social Gerontology, Clark Tibbetts ed., Chicago, University of Chicago Press, 1960. He also feels that prerogatives and participation are also important desires. In the world of Mayfair, for the more active residents, rest and participation were at times mutually exclusive.

3. This is problematic, too, because the more staff there is, the more they will tend to "run things" and remove initiative from the residents. However, if there were more staff to help residents it might take away some of the excessive importance of the few who are there now.

4. In this instance Goffman is discussing behavior in public. There are, however, in this retirement hotel some features which resemble his "total institution" as described in Asylums: Essays on the Social Situation of Mental Patients and Other Inmates, Garden City, New York, Anchor Books Doubleday and Co., Inc., 1961. All aspects of life are carried out at the hotel under the authority of staff and all residents are expected to participate together in the social activities. This must be considered, too, in relation to the presence of "uninvolved" people at social events. They may actually have nowhere else to go.

CHAPTER IV

INFORMAL SOCIAL LIFE

The planned social life at Mayfair House is
based upon planned social events which residents may
choose to attend or not as they wish. However, they
are strongly encouraged to attend. The informal
social life here has an entirely different character.
Unlike the planned social life, events have no names,
and the character of any social event of the informal
sort is more dependent upon the <u>location</u> of the event
within the Mayfair Hotel than upon any other single
factor.1 Through time, the different public areas
in the hotel have become associated with different
groups of people, and there is shared consensus
about the type of activities which take place in
these different locations. The feeling that certain
areas "belong" to certain groups is very strong and
many residents say firmly that they "never go into"
certain rooms.

This is one of the problems for the new resident
who, until he or she has friends to "clue" him or her
as to where to go, will have to discover by trial
and error which areas are which. This is often a
difficult process as the presence of a stranger in
any area is usually met with stares. The stranger
usually feels uncomfortable everywhere and only
later finds that some areas are less uncomfortable
than others.

On the ground floor opening onto the lobby
are the most popular public rooms--the Card Room,
the gift shop, the Theatre Room, and the Greenhill
Lounge. In the basement below are the Sewing Room,
Meeting Room, and Crafts Room. The Chapel and laundry
are also found on the basement level. The basement
rooms are not as popular as the upstairs rooms because of the stairs and because about 80% of the
time there is a dampness which is uncomfortable and

and irritating to arthritis sufferers. This dampness
is worse in the springtime. In the spring of 1975
there was water seeping through the carpet most of
the time and a musty smell made it almost impossible
to use the basement for any social activities.

The upstairs public rooms are the most important
ones. The Card Room and the Greenhill Lounge provide
the most striking contrast. The Card Room is a
pleasant room with southern exposure, gold curtains,
and a red and gold patterned carpet. Even on very
dark days it is bright and cheerful. A number of
card tables with comfortable chairs beside them are
scattered about the room. A few people can always
be seen playing cards, but this room functions much
more as a club than as a place for card games. It
is a lounge area for a group of residents who spend
the major part of each day there.

The majority of Card Room "regulars" are men,
but a few women sit here and there is no idea that the
area belongs to the men. Some women residents do
not like to go in there because of the thick smoke
from cigarettes and cigars, and because there are
"too many men" in there. There is usually a great
deal of talking going on there, punctuated with loud
laughter. There seems to be a great deal of discussion about age and money going on constantly. Every
time I spent a couple of hours in the card room, the
conversation went something like this:

    Mr. Brown: (in answer to a question about how he
               likes living at Mayfair:
    There are a lot of wonderful people here. But
    some have lost their brain--you know what I
    mean. They don't know where they are!

    Mr. Weitz:
    There is an old man--never knows his room
    number. I have to take him to his room
    all the time.

    Mr. Brown:
    They're old! Maybe they don't have their
    health. Yeah, that's important, it's not
    just age that does it. No! Do you know
    how old I am ?

Teski:
    No, I'm not good at guessing.

(Lots of guesses came from the group, also lots of
  laughter and jokes.)

    Mr. Brown:
        84.

    Mr. Weitz:
        That's nothing special. Guess how old I am.

    Teski:
        I don't know, but 65 or 70?

    Mr. Weitz:
        No, I'm 88 years old! I don't have wrinkles
        and I don't look it. What's more, I have my
        brain!

(General cries of "That's more than some people can
  say.")

    Mr. Brown:
        Some of the people here give you some crazy
        stories.

    Mr. Weitz:
        Yeah, they move in on Monday and by Thursday
        they're millionaires.

    Mr. Brown:
        Money, Money, Money! That's all some people
        talk about.

    Mr. Weitz:
        These people! They are just full of talk.

A further discussion about money ensued, with more
people joining in. Family and particularly what one's
children do for a living is another very popular
subject of conversation in the card room. Most of
the participants in the discussion are men who are
quite alert. Some of them may have unusual opinions
which they freely express. However, almost all of
the men who habitually sit in the Card Room accept
one another as rational people. A few rather senile-
seeming residents may wander into the Card Room and
sit idly or else go to sleep. However, these few
are looked upon with great disfavor by the livelier

group who consider that the Card Room is the place for "our kind of people." When the more <u>active</u> residents of Mayfair who are not habitual Card Room people need to sit somewhere because they are waiting to be picked up or to go in to lunch, they often sit at the front of the Card Room near the door. They are welcomed by the regulars because they are "our kind of people."

Discussion with the regular inhabitants of the Card Room almost always elicited comparisons between the Card Room and the Greenhill Lounge. Card Room habitees see the Greenhill Lounge as a kind of repository for senile-seeming and sometimes repulsive old women. Just as the Card Room is mainly used by men, the Greenhill Lounge is mainly used by women, although some men do sit there. It is a large lounge with chairs arranged about the walls and a few in the center. A small lounge within the larger one is used as a television room. The Lounge is pleasantly furnished, but the main impression which strikes one upon entering is one of silence. It is very quiet there. Many women sit in easy chairs and sleep. Conversation is carried on almost in whispers and every new arrival is greeted with stares from everyone who is not asleep.

The Lounge is controversial for both residents and staff alike, and numerous efforts have been made in the past to do something to change the sleepy atmosphere, and to make the Lounge a place where all of the residents would enjoy sitting. There are two schools of thought among the residents as to the character of the Greenhill Lounge. Some call it "the funeral parlor" and maintain that the people who habitually sit there are more dead than alive. Many residents feel that only the most senile people sit in there all day. A lively Card Room devotee said: "I never go into the Greenhill Lounge because there is a strong smell of urine there. [2] Some of the people who sit in there never even bother to go to the rest rooms." This opinion was held by a number of other residents, who regarded the room as a kind of "nursing home area." Some residents complained of a lack of modesty in some of the women who went to sleep in the Lounge and didn't notice when their dresses pulled up high. [3] Mr. Schwartz said, "I can't go in there. What I see turns my stomach." His opinion was also shared by many other residents.

The other aspect of the Greenhill Lounge is that it is considered to be a hotbed of gossip. The name applied to it in this respect is "the snake pit." Those who think of the Lounge in this way say that the people who sit there spend their time inventing or spreading vicious stories about their fellow residents. It is considered to be a place where people with nothing better to do go to hear the latest stories and perhaps add to them. Like the Card Room, the Lounge has its clubby aspects. There are people who always sit in the same seats and who are likely to say "You're sitting in my seat" to anyone else who tries to sit there. Since there are a limited number of seats it is hard for anyone new to find a place to sit. If anyone wanders in and looks around he is likely to be asked, "Are you looking for someone?" He is then expected to state his business and depart fairly soon. Observation of the group in the Greenhill Lounge over several months did show that it is populated mainly by the less active women of the hotel. No really lively resident would even consider sitting in there for any length of time. It was thought to be a place where people wasted their time, and sitting there was a sign that one was really through with life in a meaningful sense. [4] The statement "she sits in the Greenhill Lounge all day" was the worst thing that the active residents could say about someone.

Of interest is the fact that, because the Greenhill Lounge is the only true lounge at Mayfair, it is the one used for receptions for guest speakers and entertainers. It is here that the buffet with cake and coffee is set up. These parties produced a strange effect upon many of the habitual sitters in the Lounge. First of all, like most of the residents they are happy when an occasion occurs at which refreshments are served, but, on the other hand, they do not like the invasion of their usual peaceful territory by other residents who normally never come in. Every reception produces mixed reactions among the Lounge "regulars" who sit about enjoying the refreshments but also act as if they wished everyone would leave. On these occasions, of course, there is no question of protecting one's usual chair. People sit anywhere they can find a place. Many take cake or cookies in a paper napkin and go to their rooms, complaining audibly that no one could enjoy refreshments in all that confusion.

Like the Greenhill Lounge, the gift shop has a definite character. It is a "hangout" for rather active and articulate residents. It is run by a woman who is younger than most of the residents and who has a very lively and dominant personality. She travels and goes freely about the city and talks a great deal about her activities. Many residents who help out in the gift shop or go in to chat are those who are more active--even if only in spirit. Men, as well as women, can be found in the gift shop talking at all times. It is one of the few areas, like the patio, where there seems to be no predominance of one sex over the other.

Part of the reason that the gift shop has attrac ed some of the livelier residents is that it is, in a real sense, a chance for them to work at something which is more a real job than any of the committees or other activities. [5] There is real buying and selling going on, and the shop provides residents with small necessities as well as with cards and gift For many residents who rarely go outside, life withou the gift shop would be impossible. The gift shop fulfills a very useful function and those who are associated with it are well aware of the convenience they are providing for other residents. Running the gift shop is not merely "busy" work, and thus it attracts people who like to feel that they are part of the outside world with its business orientation.

Almost all residents use the gift shop for buyin small necessities, but it is rare to see a resident who is not alert and interested in conversation linge inside after making purchases. Those who stay around to talk are those who feel that they are the people who "do things" for the other residents, and who consider themselves to be more active than most of the other residents. Actually, there were some very active residents who avoided the gift shop because they did not care for the woman who was running it, but theirs was an active avoidance of the area. They did not simply leave the gift shop quickly because they felt that they had nothing to say. The very fact that the running of the gift shop causes con- troversy, and that some people have strong feelings about the group in charge shows that is is an area of activity which attracts lively people.

Working in the gift shop was, for some, a de- sirable thing which was difficult to achieve. One woman said:

> I have always wanted to work in the gift shop.
> I go there to help out whenever they need me.
> But the group that is running it always try to
> shut me out. They want to keep it all to
> themselves.

She went on to make some veiled charges of anti-
Semitism against the gift shop people. It did not
appear that such charges were true. Rather, it seemed
that the woman who spoke was a strong willed person
who had probably clashed with the strong willed
woman in charge of the gift shop who then tried to
exclude her from this desirable field of activity.
In all aspects of activity at Mayfair House, there
were only a few places for dominant, active, and
strong willed people, and sometimes the battles to
hold these places were terrible。 It is sufficient
to say here that the limited power available to Mayfair House residents acts to make residents with a
little power sometimes eager to limit the access to
power of other residents.

The gift shop provided an opportunity for real
work and a pleasant setting for spending one's time.
Therefore, access to working there or spending much
time there was limited to livelier residents who
could how their "right" to be there and also could
get along with the group who were in control of the
shop. More docile residents, and those who were
confused received no encouragement to stay and chat
in the gift shop. They made their purchases and
left, as did the lively residents who "couldn't take"
the gift shop group.

The Theatre Room is a much more neutral public
room. It is the place where almost all entertainments for the entire hotel are held. The weekly
travelogues, speakers, and musical programs are held
here. The weekly talks by the Administrator are held
here. Therefore, this area cannot "belong" to any
special group. As the Theatre Room is close to the
entrance to the Dining Room, many residents sit there
in the few minutes before the doors are opened for
meals. Anyone who wishes to do so can also sit
there and talk or doze at any time during the day. More
than any other public room it has the character of
an impersonal room. There is no group who is "always"
there although there are some residents who try to

claim certain seats when entertainments are held. One woman who always liked to sit in the back left section on the aisle told a new resident who had sat down there, "That's my seat." The new resident moved, looking puzzled and asking several other people if the seats were reserved. Another time the same woman said the same thing to an old resident who merely stared back and did not move. The woman then seated herself elsewhere remarking loudly about "Everyone knows I always sit in that seat and they just took it to be mean." Thus, any claims by individuals or groups to the Theatre Room are likely to be ignored. It is an area which is acknowledged by everyone to be for the use of everyone. During certain events, some individuals or groups may come to the forefront, but by and large it is neutral territory unlike all of the other public rooms at Mayfair. It may be that there is just too much general traffic through the room to make it attractive as a private province. Also, its lack of coziness makes it an unattractive place to be except for a specific entertainment or meeting. In the time of the research, there were no battles for the Theatre Room and there were no complaints that the use of it was dominated by any one group.

Although there are several attractive public rooms in the basement of the building, as we have said their use is limited in warmer weather because of the extreme dampness there. There is a fine billiards room, a craft room, a sewing room, a meeting room furnished with garden furniture, and a laundry. None of these rooms is attractive to the residents for enough of the year to make it worthwhile for any group to "claim" it. The billiard room actually "belonged" to the one or two players who used it each day, but there was very little interest in attending any meeting in any of the basement rooms. Important meetings were always held in the Theatre Room. The response to any gathering in the basement was always lukewarm.

The lobby, as has been mentioned, was most uninviting because of the lack of chairs. Only the most determined "hangabout" could spend much time in an area so obviously designed to discourage people from lingering. The reception desk, however, was a kind of focal point at times. The woman who ran the gift shop sometimes also acted as the switchboard operator. Her friends from the gift shop often stopped at the reception desk to chat, and sometimes a fairly large group could be found here. The reception desk was, at all times, an information center and people would stop by, whoever was on the switchboard to see "what is going on." Obviously the person at the switchboard would know important news—such as who had visitors and who had gone to the hospital or returned from the hospital. Packages for the residents are kept at the switchboard desk, and all who enter Mayfair House must stop here, so it is a good place to stay if it is information that one is seeking. Many residents make a practice of stopping by to ask if any messages have been left for them. Stopping by also gives them a chance to collect all sorts of miscellaneous information. The lobby, then, is an area through which people and rumors flow and where few people remain for long. It is a difficult, if not impossible area to claim. Like the Theatre Room, it belongs to everyone, though perhaps a bit more to the special friends of the switchboard operators. It is an area where visitors may stand without feeling that they are intruding, and where, since there are no chairs, interaction is of short duration.

The patio, in summer, like the Theatre Room and lobby, belongs to all the residents. It is the most pleasant place for sitting in warm weather as it is closed off from the street and has a nice variety of small trees and flowers. One problem is the fact that there are never enough seats for everyone who wants to sit there and some people wander out time and again looking in vain for a chair. There were complaints that some people were trying to monopolize certain chairs, but the feeling that the patio is for all is too strong to allow any such claim to be very serious. The chairs were arranged in larger groups, in small groups, and singly, so an individual could have a choice about how much company he wished to have. Throughout the summer it became clear that the same areas of the patio tended to be occupied by the same people, and new people moving into the area were likely to be stared at. However, the desirability of the patio was so great that every resident who was able to put in an appearance, did so, usually sitting wherever he could find a seat, and occupying the seat as long as he wished.

One unusual feature of the patio was that it provided a place where the very socially isolated residents seemed to feel comfortable and could "be with" people without any overt interaction going on. One man who, during the cooler months had stood

56

either in the lobby or outside the hotel door looking completely out of touch with any activity, more
or less took up residence on a single bench in the
patio when spring came. He still did not speak to
anyone, read anything, or engage in any visible
activity, but his air of having no place to go
disappeared. 6 He seemed to be at home on that bench
on the patio. It was an area where he felt comfortable sitting because it did not "belong" to anyone
in particular, and because no particular sort of interaction was expected of him if he sat there. Even in
the Theatre Room, another fairly neutral area, participation in something could be expected of those sitting there at any time. On the patio one was free
to sit and enjoy nature with no need to speak or
even "see" anybody. Therefore, for the true isolates
among the residents, it was a haven of peace outside
their rooms.

When a new resident joins Mayfair House, it is
of the utmost importance to his future social life
which areas he chooses for spending the largest
proportion of his time. This, and the type of participation he displays in regard to the planned
activities, allow the other residents to "place"
him as to the type of resident he is going to be, and
to build up a set of expectations concerning his behavior. Although it is not impossible, it is difficult
to change one's behavior after the initial patterns
of expectation have been set up, because the residents tend to interpret everything in terms of the
initial set of expectations.

In fact, several residents have undergone striking changes. One woman who came to Mayfair with a
definite drinking problem, and a real sense of despair,
had in one year conquered the problem and become
one of the most important and responsible residents.
Other people looked to her for leadership and for
help. She was consulted by the staff on many matters,
and was to them the image of what they wished all
Mayfair residents could be. She was almost universally liked and admired. Even so, some residents
could not resist mentioning to new people that she
"used to drink" and voicing the question whether a
person who had had that problem could "ever really
give it up." Thus, the past, even when it is not
really relevant to the present comes into residents'
opinions and expectations of each other. Initial impressions disappear only when all of the people who
had them disappear from the hotel, and this is why the

57

first few weeks of an individual's stay at Mayfair are crucial.

Almost every resident who discussed their first few weeks at Mayfair said that it was a time of difficulty and emotional disturbance. Although many of the residents came after their own decisions to do so, to change a way of life suddenly, especially in old age, is a hard thing to do, and many residents complained of feeling disoriented. This change, and the fact that they are for all practical purposes determining the shape of their future social life at Mayfair, make the first weeks of residence tense.

Formally, there are a number of steps taken which begin the integration of the individual into the life at Mayfair. First of all, each resident is given a room, and his or her possessions are moved in. The people on either side of the room, at least, are aware that someone new has come. Waiting for the elevator, he or she will meet other neighbors from his floor. A dining room place will be assigned to the new resident, and this is of the utmost importance, for a large proportion of the day will be spent with his table companions at the three meals. The social director is the person who make table assignments and changes table assignments. She tries to put compatible people together. Nevertheless, there is a great deal of table changing and some people have been moved from table to table in a regular circuit of the dining room. There are some people who are so unpleasant or "out of it" that no one wishes to sit with them, and since all tables are for four or more people, this presents a problem for the social director. When a new person arrives at Mayfair she tries to put him at a table which will be pleasant for him, so the table companions are probably the first people that a new resident will get to know well.

How the new resident "settles into" the dining room is probably the first clue that the residents and staff have as to the type of group member he or she will be. If there are complaints from the table mates or from the newcomer as to the satisfaction of the dining room situation, it is possibly a first warning that there will be difficulties. On the other hand, it may simply mean that the social director has made a big mistake and has put him with an impossible group of people. Many of the residents

58

have felt compelled to change their tables at one time or another.

New residents are encouraged to attend all social affairs and meetings, and are sometimes shown about by older residents. Once a month there is a newcomer tea at which all the new people who have moved in during the past month are introduced. This tea is very popular because good pastries are served to all who come. However, during the research, it was decided that too many people were coming "just to eat," and attendance was limited to the newcomers and the welcoming committee. This decision, although probably sound economically, appeared to be not so wise from the point of view of the newcomers. At the old teas where everyone was welcome, the new resident had a chance to see and be seen by more people, which helped shorten the length of time that he would be considered a stranger.

At the tea, the newcomers are given a chance to speak to the group after being introduced. They can talk about themselves, their former careers, their families, or any other safe subject.

A man who began to criticize some of the staff during his "speech" at a newcomer's tea was interrupted and told that "this is a happy occasion and we don't want to discuss such things" by the social director. Several residents also said "shhhhh!" when he began to speak in that way. Newcomers are expected to say how nice the hotel is and how nice the residents are, give any personal data they wish, and then let the next person speak.[7] The spirit of the occasion demands cheerfulness and it is usually quite cheerful except when individuals do not follow the cues they are given or occasionally begin to talk about their own troubles. The tea is a chance for at least some of the older residents to make a judgement as to how the newcomers will fit in and what kind of behavior can be expected of them. Talk of any eccentric behavior at a newcomer's tea goes around the hotel very quickly.

The problem of building a social life at Mayfair House is a serious one because, first, as we have mentioned, an individual is quickly "classified" by the other residents who then develop a set of expectations about his behavior which may or may not correspond to reality, and second, all this classification goes on during the first six or so weeks of residence when the new person may be in a state of considerable emotional upheaval. One woman who was to become later a great favorite said: "I spent my first two weeks here in my room crying over what had happened between my daughter and me." She had been forced to leave her daughter's home suddenly when the deteriorating relationship between them came to the point that the daughter demanded more "board" from her mother than the mother was able to pay, and so, heartbroken, with the help of a daughter-in-law and a niece, she had found Mayfair House where, with Public Aid, she was able to live. After the first weeks of shock wore off, she became cheerful, interested in everything, and generally a joy to have around. She was always cheerful, with unshakeable good will, but none of these qualities would have been visible during her first weeks at Mayfair.

The first six weeks seem to be the crucial time period for determining how the individual will establish relations with others and a routine for himself in the context of the life of the hotel. Unless the individual is extremely outgoing, he tends to be "invisible" for the first two weeks as far as the hotel life is concerned. During this time he may meet a few people, but he is not generally known by everyone, even by sight. In this period the new resident is settling into his room, making his own personal adjustment to a new environment--and simply coping with a large number of new impressions. After about two weeks the new resident may participate in a newcomer's tea, becoming much more "visible." After this, if he participates in meetings and comes to the entertainments, he will begin to be greeted each time by people who know him. For a few weeks every newcomer who is beginning to be known will receive extra attention--people will go out of their way to greet him or to start conversations with him. After about six weeks the extra attention will stop, the new person will become one of the regulars, and neither he nor anyone else will consider him "new" anymore.

It is in the first six weeks that a new resident establishes either an isolated or a group activity pattern for himself. Some residents come to Mayfair knowing the life style they will establish, while others feel their way alone, and arrive at something

by trial and error. Some individuals come to
Mayfair expecting a lively social life, only to
withdraw and become isolates after a few weeks.
One woman, firmly established as an isolate, said:
"I had hoped to find friends here, but there isn't
anyone who is interested in the same things I am,
so I prefer to stay in my room, read my books, and
not get involved with some of the things that go
on here. I just keep to myself and I don't get
hurt." She talks with the women at her table during
meals, but has never done any additional socializing.
She has never come to meetings and to few, if any,
entertainments. It is obvious from what she has
said of her past life that she was following a
pattern which she established long before coming to
Mayfair, but felt that she had to justify it by
saying that she had looked in vain for people with
whom she could socialize. Another man, obviously a
sociable person, seemed to have established himself
as an isolate after a very real search for people
to talk with. He said: "When I cam here I really
looked for people to talk with. I talked to everyone! They won't talk to me now because they are
suspicious of my political ideas (socialist). They
say I want to destroy the government of the United
States, and I don't! I just want to talk about
some ideas, but they don't have any ideas. I'm not
an educated person, but I have read. These people
don't know who Tolstoy is. They don't know who
Marx is! They don't know anything. I get disgusted.
I have no one to talk to so I stay alone." In fact,
this man was always trying to find people to talk
with and he engaged almost every newcomer in conversation. He said he had given up on finding friends,
but actually he was always trying to find them. Unlike the woman described earlier, he was involved in
an on-going search, and was not happy with his
position as an isolate.

On the other hand, many people, especially women,
who had been rather isolated in their own homes or
in the homes of their children found a sudden
blossoming of social life after they moved into
Mayfair. Many women who had come from Europe in
the early part of the century and had been solely
engaged in housework and caring for children, found
a chance to meet more different types of people at
Mayfair House. A very active woman put it this
way: "My son invites me to his house often, and I
like to go to see my grandchildren, but he lives
in the suburbs and there's nothing for me to do but

61

sit and watch the television. I have no one to
talk to. Here I see lots of people. I have friends
here who are old, like me. They understand the
problems I have. I also do a lot of work for committees. Too much work! I get tired, but I don't get
so bored. It's better than sitting around." This
woman has found less isolation in her old age than
earlier.

Another woman who had been an active person all
of her life simply tried to continue the same pattern in her retirement at Mayfair House. She said:
"I was always active, especially in my church. I
always felt that I could help. I raised three
children and we never had much money, but I always
gave my time to try to do some service for others.
I belonged to clubs too--the women's auxiliary of
the American Legion and other clubs too. It wouldn't
have been natural for me to come here and sit. So
I joined all the committees and I help people to go
places if they need help in walking and I visit
anyone who goes to the hospital. It all gets to be
too much sometimes, but I can't say no!" She is
well liked and well integrated into the life at
Mayfair, and from what she says, retirement was not
a huge transition for her, but rather a continuation
of her way of life in a different arena.

Another woman much liked because of her unfailing
kindness and optimism, said this of her retirement:
"When I was working, I never thought of retirement
as something bad, the end. I thought of it as the
beginning of the time when I could give all of my
time to the thing which had always been most important to me, volunteer work. I never had the time to
give when I was working every day. Now for as long
as I'm here I'll be able to be of more service. And
it makes me happy! It's what I love doing!" Although she is by no means among the younger Mayfair
residents, she goes out of the hotel each day for
volunteer work and also manages to participate in
most of the meetings and almost all of the classes
which are offered, making active contributions. This
woman has become something of an institution at
Mayfair. She has become a living example of what
retirement can be--of the things which it is possible
for the active retired person to do. She is, in
fact, the only person encountered during the research
who said that she _planned_ what she was going to do

after her retirement. Most people were rather surprised by retirement and said that they had experienced a period of feeling "lost" until they found
their way into a new life.

Prepared or, most usually, unprepared for life
at a retirement hotel, the new resident is rather
quickly absorbed into the life of the hotel, or
he is seen as an isolate and not really bothered about
anymore. The staff take great pains to try to make
the new person feel at home in the first weeks he
is there. After that he is expected to take care
of himself, and no further efforts are made to
bring him into the activities. Often staff members
would say of a resident, "She never participates
in anything," with no idea of creating new activities
which some of the isolates might be drawn to participate in. If an individual does not participate at
first he will be classified by all as a non-participant and it will be harder for him to be accepted
in an active role later.

Footnotes for Chapter IV

1. There was very little of the problem of crowding (see Hall 1969) except in the use of the elevators when one or more was not working, and in adequate space in the smaller public rooms when refreshments were being served. In both of these instances, the worst types of quarrels tended to break out among residents.

2. There was at times, although not always, such a smell in this lounge. It is interesting that this area was defined by some residents as an olfactory space (Hall 1969:45-50). The connotations of the type of olfactory experience sometimes presented here was enough to keep some people out permanently.

3. This behavior by certain women turned what was supposed to be a public area into a private one and effectively barred some people from entering the room.

4. While most of the people here did not do much in the planned social life, their reputation for gossip showed a lively involvement with activities of their fellow residents—even though they were only involved as spectators.

5. Kleemeier (1954) reports for "Moosehaven" a campus like retirement facility for Moose members and their relatives, that everyone who was able to work did work for the community and that all like to work. See also Kleemeier, "Effects of Work Programs on Adjustment Attitudes of an Aged Population," Journal of Gerontology 1 (October 1951: 373-379).

6. The extra space, although there were no extra chairs in the patio, meant that his presence could not be interpreted as intrusive as long as he did not try to sit in the midst of any conversation groups.

7. Most of the newcomers say that they came to Mayfair hoping to meet new friends. G.C. Hoyt in "The Life of the Retired in a Trailer Park," American Journal of Sociology, vol. 59 (January 1954), found that sociability was an important factor among the people he studied in bringing them to the decision to move to a retirement community.

CHAPTER V

REALITY PARTICIPATION, SOCIAL INTERACTION,

AND STATUS

In the common life world of Mayfair House, there
were in fact deep divisions between individuals and
between groups of people. Months of observation led
to the formulation of the concept of the "reality
participation circle" as a device for describing the
breadth of an individual's involvement with the world
outside himself. To the extent that there was any
<u>intense</u> community feeling and social life at Mayfair,
it was mainly among people who had similar reality
participation circles. Loneliness was caused by an
individual's not finding enough people engaging in
the same type of reality that he was. Thus, he might
find himself unable to maintain his own sense of the
reality of his experience at a fully operative level.[1]
There is a need for the sharing of perceptions which
leads to the reinforcement of interpretations of
people, things, and events.

Four breadths of reality participation circle
best describe those found among the residents at
Mayfair. They have been stated in Chapter I
and we will list them again here.

(1) Individual awareness--the physical and mental
    reality of one person--his idiosyncratic
    world view and his reactions to things around
    him.

(2) Small group awareness--the reality of a few
    friends--informal conversation or gossip
    groups.

(3) Hotel social life awareness--the world of the
    planned social program--committees, dealing
    with management and staff, working with other

residents, planning events.

(4)Wider world awareness--Friends, organizations, entertainments, commitments, and communication outside the hotel.

Naturally, most of the residents operated at all these breadths of reality during their day or week, but through constant communication, it became clear that each resident thought, spoke, and acted with reference to a _particular_ reality participation circle a majority of the time. Thus, there were those who were completely immersed in experience of, and conversation about, their own physical sensations. There were those who were deeply involved with a gossip group of perhaps five members, those who saw the hotel and its social life as their main "world," and those who were thoroughly involved in events beyond the hotel. To each of these groups, their involvements represented the most persistent aspect of reality and were indeed, to them, reality itself.

The reality participation circle of any given individual was determined by having at least three separate conversations with him or her. I then wrote down the conversation and the number of times the individual mentioned his or her own sensations, other people, social events at the hotel, and events in the world outside the hotel. On the basis of what the individual talked about most in the three conversations, he or she was placed in one of the four types of reality participation circles. As we see in Figure 1, there are a number of possible loci within each circle and it is also possible to be in a transitional position between two circles.

In a hotel with people operating on so many different levels, it becomes crucial that an individual find a group of friends who affirm the same type of reality that he does. Activities and conversations with this group are the means through which an individual feels that he is part of the world--through being part of a group, however small, who agree with him as to what "the world" is. Too often at Mayfair, residents expressed extreme unhappiness at "not having anyone that I can talk with." In actual fact these people may have been talking with many others, but had found few who confirmed their own level of reality participation. Interactions often took place which left people with a sense of talking without sharing—simply because they were talking past one another in different circles.

The following dialogue is a model of a common conversation at Mayfair, a dialogue taking place with each of the participants operating in a different type of reality.

Dialogue on Three Levels

The dialogue takes place among three women sitting at a table in the dining room. They were seated at the same table by the Social Director.

Mrs. Smith: This isn't vanilla ice cream" It has nuts in it! They never have anything I like!

Mrs. Schwartz: I go to dining room committee every week and we have been trying to get the Food Director to put more of the things we like on the menu, but she never changes anything. She just listens and says she'll look into it, and does nothing!

Mrs. Smith: The nuts give me indigestion, and I have to take those little green pills from my doctor!

Mrs. Able: They are putting too many non-food additives into much of our food! Heaven knows what's in that ice cream! I have been writing to my congressman about it, and I joined a natural foods group. I think more people have to speak out against artificial and possibly dangerous things in our food!

Mrs. Smith: I like chocolate cake and chocolate ice cream.

Mrs. Schwartz: We spoke out in committee meeting again raw liver, and she promised we wouldn't get it again, but she served it two weeks later. I get frustrated trying to get things done around here.

Mrs. Able: The trouble is that there's too much
                 apathy! Even President Ford only wants
                 to have people around him who already
                 agree with him. He doesn't want to
                 bother exchanging points of view. It
                 would be good for a president to have
                 to defend his ideas once in a while.
                 Sometimes I wonder if politicians
                 have any ideas! They'll use any idea
                 they think will get them elected.

Mrs. Schwartz: "Yes" men! Yes! Our committee is full
                 of them! All they do is to tell Mrs.
                 Food Services how good everything is
                 so she'll be happy. Then she con-
                 tinues to give us stuff I wouldn't
                 give my dog! Day after day!

Mrs. Smith: Isn't that strawberry ice cream on the
                 cart there? I could eat that!
                 Waiter! Please give me a different
                 ice cream. Well! That's better! But,
                 what I'd really like is some chocolate!

     All three ladies, if asked, would have affirmed
that they had had a conversation. In fact, none of
them had spoken in the area of primary reality of the
others. Information was exchanged, but the conversation did nothing for any of the ladies in terms of
making them feel that they belonged to a group, and
it did nothing to give positive reinforcement to the
reality participation circle within which each of
them was operating.2 In the long run, conversations
like this make people more, rather than less, lonely.

     Mrs. Smith actually has in some ways the best
chance for feeling "understood" because the reality
participation circles of Mrs. Schwartz and Mrs. Able
encompass hers. Everyone has food preferences, sensations, and health difficulties of one sort or another. On another occasion, she and Mrs. Schwartz
might have a fulfilling conversation comparing their
doctors and pills. However, to Mrs. Schwartz her
activities in the hotel and the social structure
there are what is "really important," and she might
later remark that Mrs. Smith is a nice person but
"doesn't know what's going on." Mrs. Schwartz and
Mrs. Able have something in common because they are

both activists and believe that they should work for change. But Mrs. Able sees the world outside Mayfair House and the "Real World" and considers too much involvement with the committees and power struggles of the hotel as "petty" and "not worth" all the fuss. 3

Although conversations which say nothing and do nothing to give a sense that one is part of a group which shares one's feelings in some part, are the common lot of everyone at times, the problem becomes more acute in a retirement hotel. Age, the neighborhood, the weather in winter, limit the mobility of most of the residents. Financial problems also limit their mobility crucially. They are dependent upon the other residents for company most of the time. It is with the other residents that they must build a world of ideas and shared assumptions which will be for them external reality, or the world as it is.

All of the residents come to Mayfair with such a life world in their heads, but in order to maintain their sense of reality, they must have contact with others who at least share some of their modes of perception of things and events around them. Most residents have had to restructure their sense of reality to a certain extent to adapt to the new style of life at Mayfair. However, people who have habitually interacted with a small group, a community, or within a community which had wider concerns will look for others with like habits and concerns (operating within reality participation circles 2,3,4). Those who have been involved with a circle 1 reality participation (individual) will probably not change.

A new resident was discussing her first impressions. She said she was very unhappy and displeased with the life at Mayfair. When she was asked why, she began by saying that she didn't like the food and that her room was not very nice. She added that those are the most important factors in determining whether a person will or will not like a place. She gave detailed descriptions of what she didn't like about the food and about her room. She was then aske if she liked the people. At this question she looked surprised, as if someone had asked something complete ly irrelevant and said something vague which showed that she had not even thought about the other residents and didn't know whether she liked them or not

It seemed unlikely that she would make very great changes in her reality participation circle in the future. She maintained distance from most of the other residents throughout the research.

A person's social life or lack of social life is also dependent upon how they perceive the hotel and the other residents. A great deal depends upon what the individuals believe to be possible in the way of social contact. A Hungarian woman whose English was very good seemed terribly lost and isolated. She would come into the office to talk from time to time, but she never seemed to talk much with the other residents. She appeared to be very depressed. She was constantly coming in to give reports on how lonely and depressed she is. She is 75 years old but she is lively and seemingly healthy, and yet new relationships are not part of her world of possibilities. When asked about the hotel and the residents she made it clear that she was not living in a retirement hotel but in an "old folks home." That was what she called it and that is the way she thinks of it. She also thinks of the residents as "old folks" and has very definite beliefs about what it is to be among "old folks." For example, "old folks" are always ill and they are always lost in their own thoughts and problems and have no time for anyone else. For this reason, her loneliness, from her point of view, is inevitable. She is quite full of ideas and opinions when talking with younger people, but believes that it is impossible to really talk with "old folks." Pointing out that she is old and that she likes to talk about things other than her aches and pains did not convince her. She is firmly convinced that she must be lonely because everyone is lonely in an "old folks home."

Therefore, the first requisite of establishing some sort of social contact is to believe that it is possible. Secondly, it is necessary to make contact with at least a few people who are operating within a similar reality participation circle. If this is possible, the individual can begin to build a "world" within a world which will be familiar and somewhat satisfying to him. There were a few men who said very little but habitually sat in the card room. They took no part in the games or jokes there, but they were accepted by the others who recognized them as "regulars" and did not stare when they came in. Although they appeared to be participating very

little, they were part of the "world" of the card room.
People would have noticed if one of them did not appear. They were members of a small community within
the larger community of the hotel, and belonging to
this community gave all members, even those who were
not as active as others, a sense of reality of experience and a sense that there was somewhere to go to
spend the day.

One characteristic of the real isolates is that
they seem to have nowhere to go. They go from room
to room, perhaps staying a few minutes and then moving on. They are more often seen passing through the
front lobby than are residents who are usually engaged
in social activities, and therefore have someplace
to go. They are not part of any of the groups which
"own" certain areas, and it is hard for an individual
to claim any area other than his own room. The isolates appear to be very restless, often wandering
away even during an entertainment. They seem like
strangers in the hotel, although some of them have been
residents for years. In fact, the isolated individual
is a stranger. Other residents have become used to
seeing him and they have learned to ignore him. He
is ignored because the word has gotten around that it
is not possible to socialize with him, so after a
time, no one tries. Early in the research, I found
that I was being informed that certain people were
"impossible to talk with" even though many of them
were eager to talk. The more often one talked with
the "impossible to talk to" people, the more other
residents would come round to tell anecdotes which
proved that these people were impossible. In fact,
many of them were difficult personalities whose
circle #1 world view was enough to distract from the
reinforcing purposes of any group. Many of them were
very lucid, but with so bizarre an approach to social
life that they were very upsetting to the other residents. A woman who liked to keep birds and who felt
toward them as a mother, was widely shunned and referred to as "Batty" and worse. Actually, she was
mildly eccentric, but in the context of Mayfair House
where social contacts are restricted largely to the
residents, she was seen as a threat to everyone's
sense of reality. She was very much an isolate, but
seemed to want to be part of the activities at times.
If they had been in a more supportive (of their own
reality participation circle) environment, many
people who had avoided her might have seen her as an
odd but amusing companion. It is not a tolerant

atmosphere at Mayfair. People try to find people who agree with them and support their own ideas about things. Others are perceived as dangerous--"not the sort of people who ought to be here."[4]

It is all too hard for individuals at Mayfair to find others who are operating within their same reality participation circle and who also have a few ideas in common. A new man came to Mayfair operating very much in circle 4. He was interested in the world outside Mayfair and was also very interested in the workings of the world of Mayfair itself. He made contact with many other individuals also operating at circle 4. He was outgoing and liked to talk, but within a week or two he had made several enemies among the circle 4 people because of differences of opinion. He reported after about three weeks that he liked life at the hotel fairly well, but that there were several people that he "couldn't stand." All of the people he mentioned were outstanding circle 4 operators who would be that group among which he should have found most of his friends. By having quarreled with them and deciding that they were "idiots" he cut himself off from a source of reinforcement for his own sense of reality. Later he found a small group of circle 4 people whom he did not consider "idiots." The points of difference of opinion were so strong that they distracted his attention from the fact that these people with whom he was disagreeing were at least agreeing with him as to what the important things to discuss were.

Over the period of the research, it became obvious that the people operating in circle 1 were actually the least happy because naturally there was no one who really shared their main concern-- their own problems. People who operated within reality participation circles 2,3, or 4 had a better chance of finding what they perceived to be a satisfying life. Certainly they were not so isolated. Those operating within circles 3 and 4 often objected to the presence of people in circles 1 and 2 at the hotel because they felt that the hotel was "not a nursing home" and they objected to having people who were "out of it" or "just sitting around gossiping" living with them. They felt that it gave the place a bad atmosphere and that the presence of these people meant that there would not be places

for more lively people who might apply for admittance.
They also felt that the fact that there were so many
circle 1 and 2 people might discourage livelier
people from coming to Mayfair if they came for a
visit of inspection and saw too many"out of it"
people or too many passive gossip groups. Over and
over, people displayed a cynicism about the admittance policies of the hotel. People felt that the
owners were just out to make money and were not at
all selective about the people that they admitted.
Almost no one believed the rhetoric about the careful selection of residents. There was a rumor that
there were no longer even very real standards of
physical capability required. In fact, some of the
residents were so unsteady that they had to have a
visiting nurse come to supervise their baths. Many
of the healthier and livelier residents felt that
there was too much burden being put on them to look
after people who really could not manage on their
own. One of the big problems was that many of the
residents needed to take certain medications during
the day and would not remember their doses. There
was a strict policy that the staff did not involve
itself with medication.[5] What happened, if a person
were lucky, was that another resident would take it
upon himself to remind him about his medications.
This is actually a nice case of mutual help. However,
many of the residents who reminded others about their
medicines felt a strong resentment towards the staff
because this was necessary. They felt that the
staff should either have someone to help about medication, or not admit people who were unable to be
responsible. Often this complaint was heard: "I
don't mind asking Mabel if she has taken her heart
pill, but I worry. What if I don't feel well one
day, and can't go looking for her. What happens
then? I'm old too, and my health isn't the best.
I don't feel I should have the responsibility."

The sense of responsibility for the less capable
residents, along with the fear that others would
"think I'm like them" makes it difficult for the
residents who would love to see everyone operating
in reality circles 3 and 4. It weakened their tolerance for these people, and gave them a feeling
of frustration and "not being at home" at Mayfair.
The lack of tolerance among many of the residents
was one of the outstanding facts which emerged in
the months of research. The circle 1 and 2 people
were probably already not terribly tolerant, be-

cause their interest in other people was limited.
The circle 3 and 4 people had their tolerance weakened by the feeling that they had too much responsibility for the other residents. One woman said:
"I'm retired too. I'm supposed to be taking it easy,
but I get so upset. There are people here who don't
know whether they have eaten or not. See that man
there? He was sitting at our table at lunch, and he
had already eaten at the earlier sitting. I tried
to convince him, but he wouldn't leave. Then the
Food Service Director made him leave and he cried
and said he was hungry. That happens about every
two days. We try to tell him, but he won't listen."
The speaker was frustrated. She felt sorry for the
man, but his continual mistakes about meals were
making her life difficult and she resented it.

The tension between people with vastly different
reality participation circles, and the intolerance
resulting from this tension was the most important
social problem perceived at Mayfair during the research. It is this which made it difficult for real
community to be established among all of the residents
and it weakened their experience of the shared life
world. The lack of identity with one another which
many residents felt pulled Mayfair apart as a potential community rather than uniting it. Being old
simply was not enough to create community.

Interviews, casual conversations, and observation established that the residents were divided
into roughly two groups. About 30% of the residents
were operating on circle 3 and 4 and about 70%
on circle 1 and 2, with more of this half on circle
1 than on circle 2. This means that about 30% of
the residents were sometimes resentful of the fact
that the other 70% "did not participate," "couldn't
take care of themselves," "weren't useful," or
"should be in a nursing home." These figures are
only an approximation, but it was confirmed numeri-
cally to a certain extent by counting the people
who came to the meetings, entertainments, and classes, and comparing the number with what was observed,
and what residents said about who did and who did
not participate.

It is much harder to try to speculate about why
any given individual was involved in a particular
reality participation circle. Surely the factors
are multiple and they include: health, former life
style, education, former occupation, command of

74

English, and the way the individual feels about living in a retirement hotel. Also important is the way in which the individual perceives the other residents at the hotel. His response will be different if he regards them as companions or potential companions, than if he thinks of them as "old folks" not to be bothered about. All of these elements go into the establishment by the individual of a pattern of daily activity which will, through time, create for him a reality participation circle and a place in the social structure.

A person's position in the social hierarchy at Mayfair House was linked importantly with his reality participation circle. When people were asked who the important people were at the hotel, a few names would come up over and over again. The names were always those of people who were very active in social life and who had the respect of the staff. Conversation with these important residents revealed that they were always participating in reality circles 3 and 4. One hundred people were asked directly whom they considered to be "important" at the hotel and at least fifty others opinions were collected casually through conversation. The same names always emerged.

As we shall discuss more completely later, the important residents gained much of their prestige through the extra respect given them by staff and by their functions as unofficial staff members. Through their contacts with staff they were closer than the other residents to the sources of power, and the extra regard of staff put them in a better position for determing their own activities in a satisfactory way.

Involvement with the world, at least in a circle 3 and 4 type participation, was necessary in order to bring the individual into social situations in which he could begin to build up some kind of influence over other people. Only circle 3 or 4 people had the particular focus of interest necessary for sustained social activity in this sphere. Circle 1 and 2 people and a few circle 4 people did not find this level of social interaction possible or meaningful. Access to a favorable position in the social hierarchy, then was distinctly limited to persons with the appropriate reality participation circles, and the disposition to cooperate with staff

Footnotes for Chapter V

1. Lack of a "reference group" (Shibutani 1967) or dependence upon an "orientational other" (Kuhn 1967) which is not present at the hotel, is another way of expressing this situation. However, the idea of breadth of reality participation more readily indicates the total "world" which every individual in society carries with him.

2. Patterns of meaning belong to different groups within a culture. Hall (1973) describes this well in discussing non-verbal behavior: "The individuals of a group share patterns that enable them to see the same thing and this holds them together" (1963:123). However, there are so many different levels of interpretation of the "same thing" that groups within groups are formed. This is what the concept of reality participation circle describes.

3. Goffman, in The Presentation of the Self in Everyday Life (1959), discusses mechanisms of face-to-face interaction. In an interaction each individual projects a definition of the situation and usually these definitions are compatible enough so that direct contradictions don't occur. However, as in this conversation, the definitions projected by the different participants (in this case the three women) might be just different enough to throw the conversation slightly "off"--making it unsatisfactory to each of them.

4. Ernest W. Burgess (1954) analyzed the social relations at Mooschaven (see Kleemeier 1954) and found three major divisions among the people there. There were: (1) Isolates; (2) Intimates--people with a few friends; and (3) Leaders--who interacted with many people. There were two kinds of Isolates-- Isolates by bilateral exclusion and Isolates by unilateral exclusion. At Mayfair House, both of these types of Isolates were noticed.

5. This one factor was important to staff as an indication that Mayfair House was "not an institution." They would say with pride that "people here take care of themselves."

76

CHAPTER VI

THE CREATION AND MAINTENANCE OF SHARED REALITY

In the previous chapter we discussed the obstacles to the creation of community at Mayfair. As we say, the fact that residents functioned on a number of different reality participation circles was the main social problem. Community then, in its stricter sense, is created, not in the entire population of the hotel, but among smaller groups of the residents. People who have similar reality participation circles tend to form groups which reinforce their views of reality. Such groups give them people to talk with whom they know will strengthen their own views of the world. The existence of such groups is the only protection against extreme loneliness for the Mayfair residents. What one finds there is a series of communities within the larger grouping, or life world.

Berger (1963,1969) deals definitively with the problem of reality as created by society, both in the larger sense of the reality of an entire culture and in the more limited sense of the reality of the individual and small group.

> The individual, then, derives his world view socially in very much the same way that he derives his roles and his identity. In other words, his emotions and his self interpretation like his actions are predefined for him by society, and so is his cognitive approach to the universe that surrounds him(1963:117).

This sense of reality is a continuing creation throughout the lifetime of the individual, although the type of perceptions he is likely to employ may be very firmly set by the time he reaches old age. At this time of life a person will probably seek out a group with which he feels comfortable and whose general perception of reality agrees with his own. Berger discusses this under the topic of "reference groups." He sees each such group as representing a certain approach to reality.

> Every group to which one refers oneself occupies a vantage point on the universe. Every

role has a world view dangling from its end. In choosing specific people one chooses a specific world to live in. If the sociology of knowledge gives us a broad view of the social construction of reality, reference group theory shows us the many little workshops in which cliques of universe builders hammer out their models of the cosmos (1963:120).

This is very much the case at Mayfair. We have seen that there are many cliques creating "models of the cosmos." However, the acute problem in this case, and perhaps in every human case, is that there is a limit to the number of people whom it is possible to see, and an elderly resident, used to reinforcement of reality of a certain type, may find no groups whose orientation even approximates what was encountered in earlier life. The problem is dealt with here by seeking out other residents with similar reality participation circle, but as has been said before, this is no guarantee that there will be agreement with these others on points within the circle which both have agreed is "real." This was shown by the case of the lively circle 4 operator who disagreed with many of the other circle 4 people and cut himself off from them because they were "idiots." Another very acute man, originally from Japan, said that he wished that there were "one or two Japanese people here." He also said wistfully that the food was all right but that he wished so much for rice, explaining carefully that "oriental people don't really feel that it's a meal if there's no rice." Although he was lively and interested in things, there was no one who could share his very strong feelings about the nutritional and emotional value of a bowl of rice with one's meal.

Limitation on the number of groups with which one could identify led to compromise in the case of Mayfair residents, and people tended to modify their demands and to become more like the people with whom they commonly assoicated. A new resident who may have said that there was "no one" at Mayfair for her will bit by bit search out a group or groups with similar reality participation circles and begin to share, at least in part, their interpretation of the world. This is a difficult process for a new resident and it takes some time. As we have described earlier, the first few weeks at May fair are usually a time of emotional upheaval for

the new resident. Some have even said that they
were in such a whirl that they cannot now remember
the first few weeks. Many said of the early days
at Mayfair, "It all seemed so unreal." In fact,
it was unreal for them because they had no familiar
signals around them to affirm their sense of reality.
Not identified with a group who will serve this function as yet, they are adrift and unsure of themselves.
Any problems surrounding their coming to Mayfair also weaken their sense of "what's what," leaving
them vulnerable. If they move quickly into activities and begin to see with whom they want to be
and which groups they wish to avoid, the adjustment
process is less painful.

In <u>Under the Sacred Canopy</u>, Berger (1969)
argues for the importance of conversation as a
reality confirming device. In a hotel like Mayfair,
where there is ample time for conversation, it is
critical for the creation and maintenance of reality for the various groups of residents. Conversation is the means by which individuals communicate
to one another their reality participation circles,
and determine whether another individual is operating in the same circle. It is the means by which
established groups who share the same breadth of
reality participation maintain the conceptions which
they share. Even most of the isolates at Mayfair
felt some need for conversation. A very old man,
who seemed a complete isolate and spent most of his
time standing in the hall, responded eagerly to a
"Good Morning." He did not speak a great deal of
English and he had a speech defect as well, so
communication was difficult. He would come into the
office to show his social security checks. Remarks
would be exchanged as to how nice it was that it had
come on time, etc. He would then leave and continue
standing in the hall. One day a small boy came to
the hotel and stopped to say "hello." He did not
seem to notice that the man couldn't speak very
well but went on talking to him about various children's things. Delighted, the man kept patting the
child on the head and ended by giving him 35 cents
which he very much needed himself. He wanted communication but had not, among the limited population at
Mayfair, been able to find an individual or group
with which he could establish a conversation of
any sort.

An example from my childhood will illustrate

this point. My father had a large garden and needed help with it, so he hired an elderly man from somewhere in Central Europe. He never spoke much and we though he was unable to speak. Then one day a Polish lady, who was working in the house, went out and began to try different languages that she recalled from her childhood. To the amazement of us children, she found his language and we discovered that he could, in fact, talk perfectly well. We had thought that there was something physiologically wrong with him. He had simply been cut off from a population which could have been a community for him. We had thought that he had a "condition" which cut him off from communication, when actually the external circumstances of his life had cut him off.

In life, and most especially among a limited population such as that of Mayfair, it is partly a matter of luck whether one can find a satisfactory reality affirming group. There were relatively few people at Mayfair for whom language was the major problem in establishing communication, although there were a few. Most people did find at least a few others with whom conversation was a meaningful affirmation of their own world views.

Conversation, then, was the main means by which an individual could "place" another individual as to his reality participation circle, and could locate others with similar circles to his own. Once having located a group of similar thinking individuals, conversation was the means by which the group maintained a sense of continued participation for its members--participation both in a group and in a specific breadth of reality participation. For example, the small gossip group, congregating in the Greenhill Lounge, would maintain a sense of group by trying to occupy the same chairs and by always greeting one another. The reality circle which they operated on was that of the "village gossip," and in order to keep a sense of continued participation at this level, new material has to be constantly introduced. So members watch each other and their fellow residents carefully for new information. Because there is so little going on at times, the gossip group members often have to use their imagination just to keep things going. Circulation of untrue stories was one thing which many residents complained of and often pointed to certain gossip groups as being the originators of the rumors. One man said: "I was almost destroyed and driven crazy by gossip. A couple of years ago I used to talk with a very fine woman. We were friends, and then people started saying we were going to get married. We were not planning to get married and the gossip spoiled the friendship. I never felt so bad in my life before, and I've been through a lot. Those gossips are really cruel. They shouldn't be allowed to talk the way they do."

Another man and woman had a different response, but also felt that the gossip mongers were irresponsible. They said that they regarded what was said by the gossips rather as a joke: "You would not believe what they said about us! A couple of years ago we went on separate vacations, but at the same time, the rumor was spread around that we had gone to Jamaica and had gotten married! Then we did go on a vacation on the same cruise ship, and they spread it around that we had gone to Mexico for a quick divorce! We don't let them spoil our friendship. We ignore them. It's sad because they don't have lives of their own, so they have to make up lies about other people's lives."

The gossip groups responsible for such rumors were interested in maintaining a lively flow of information about other people's lives. They had to resort to untruths at times, but often they knew the truth about things before anyone else did because of their constant observation and "snooping." When the research was begun, the Social Director had said: "Please don't pay any attention to rumors that I'm leaving. They start things going around that simply are not true." One month later she announced her intention of leaving and let it be known that she had been considering another job for some months. Interestingly enough, if the gossip groups said that someone on the staff was leaving, that person usually did leave very shortly thereafter. True rumors were much preferred by the gossip groups, as the results could be used to show their acute powers of observation.

Untrue rumors which could not easily be disproven were also popular. Talk of secret marriages and divorces and talk that "Mr. X has a million dollars in the bank: were the type of rumors which could not easily be proved or disproved, and gave a great deal of zest to conversation and a sense of really being "in on things."

Conversation, meetings, and projects were the means by which the groups who were concerned with the social life of the hotel as a whole maintained their reality participation circle. People operating at this breadth maintained a constant interest in what was going on in the hotel as a whole, and what the Mayfair residents were doing as a "community." They might well have listened to gossip group rumors, but for them the real action was in the planned activities, in trying to get staff to take up certain projects, and in feeling in touch with the operation of the whole hotel. People with this reality participation circle were likely to appear at most meetings and to speak out in meetings nearly every time they attended. Conversation among this group of people tends to be specific: "What are we going to do about people who don't use the garbage chutes in the halls?" "When are we going to have more ashtrays in the patio?" "How many people have signed up for the excursion to the museum?" etc. Typically, conversations among this group involve more questions than conversations among the small gossip groups. The conversation in the gossip group is usually statement after statement, while the circle 3 people take a more problem-oriented direction, tending to ask and to answer questions, often arguing about the answers. There is a faster pace to conversation, and a belief that it is possible to engineer change. The gossip groups, although they may, in fact, change peoples' lives with rumors, do not see themselves a change-originating group. They see themselves as observers and commentators on the passing scene.

Circle 4 people, those interested in the "outside world" as well as the world of Mayfair, are great users of conversation, both to affirm their own reality participation level with others of similar interest, and to inform everyone of their wider interests. Two very stimulating circle 4 ladies, both in their 80s, loved to bring their interests into conversation. One was learning Russian and wanted everyone to know that. The other had learned Spanish and said she planned to study "a lot of other things." The circle 4 residents are often very eager to make it clear that they are not like the other residents. Some carry newspapers around with them and point out the stories which concern them most. One woman was very interested in civic problems and tried to interest anyone she could in these.

Contacts with the people from "outside" are more important to the circle 4 people than to the other residents. One of the most active men made daily phone calls to a number of people including the president of the corporation which owns the hotel and made sure that other people knew about these calls. It is important to this group that their sphere of activity and interest does not stop at Mayfair House. They feel that they must belong to a wider community. Discussing news events, taking part in charity work in outside organizations, sponsoring speakers from the community who come to Mayfair House, getting involved in neighborhood groups, or even having a part-time job were all means through which an individual can feel himself to belong to the world of "people" rather than the world of just "retired people." Discussion of such concerns among people at this level gives a strong sense of not being "cut off" from the larger society. Those residents who were able to travel and to return and describe their trips were in a very good position. Even non-circle 4 people were eager to hear their descriptions of new places and would look at as many slides as the speaker wished to show.

The circle 4 people are only too well aware that, in a retirement hotel, it is easy to retreat from an active involvement with all except what is going on in the immediate surroundings. It is this state of things which they wish to avoid. Many stated that this is just what makes people "old."[1] In a discussion group, a woman said with obvious agitation: "Everyone should learn something every day. The reason that this place is depressing is that no one wants to learn anything new or to change their mind about anything. We have many interesting classes here, but the same people always go. The others just sit forever and think the same thoughts they have been thinking for fifty years. You see, we have a good discussion group here, but there are only ten people. The others just stay away. Sometimes I get disgusted!"

She was actually upset and afraid that if people stopped attending the discussion groups and lectures, that eventually these would no longer be held and she would lose an important source of stimulation. Those who want to maintain a sense of participating in the wider world must work hard at

it. They must leave the hotel and move about the
city. They must seek out similar individuals among
the new residents, and they must attend all of the
"worthwhile" events sponsored by the hotel, so that
they will not be discontinued. Many write accounts
of their experiences, or give opinions about something for the monthly Mayfair Newsletter. This is
compendium of stories, reports on events, poems,
and stories written by the residents. Incidentally,
the publication is edited by the social director,
who presumably selects the "best" articles for publication. One wonders why, if the articles are
written by residents, there could not also be a
resident as editor, but it is the social director
who selects the material to be printed.

It is difficult for circle 4 people to find
enough other people who can maintain with them their
type of reality participation. Therefore, these
people, although they have more sources of satisfaction than many other residents, may become more
easily disillusioned and frustrated, expressing
this in extreme lack of tolerance for their fellow
residents. Adeline Smith, a very warm-hearted
person, who did all she could to help other residents said, "You know, I used to think that
young people who ignore older people were so cruel.
Now, I ignore some of the residents here, because
otherwise, I just can't stand life. I know they
are forgetful and don't mean to keep doing and saying the same things all the time, but it's so depressing. I keep thinking--I don't want to be like
them--but if I listen to them too much I'll begin
to act the same way and I'd rather be dead. I try
not to say anything. I just try to ignore what
upsets me." She, in fact, felt that the life style
which she found satisfying could be threatened by
too much association with others who were very self-
involved and perhaps senile. During the research
it was obvious that the circle 4 people were quite
protective of their life style and tried to spend
most of their time with others who would affirm it.
Circle 3 people, involved mainly in the world of
the hotel, also sought out others with like concerns and tended to make many disparaging remarks
about "people who live here, but let others do all
the work." Often the circle 3 people were less
tolerant because they were more immediately involved
with the hotel. In many cases there were indivi-

duals who were operating well in both circles 3 and
4 most of the time. However, in conversation it
was easy to determine where their most heartily
felt concern was--with the hotel--or with the world
outside. During the research, literally hundreds of
conversations were recorded, each one showing something of the circle of reality with which the speakers were most fully involved.

There were also non-conversational means for
residents to establish a shared reality with one
another. Presence or absence in certain places and
at certain events could be very eloquent. We have
already discussed the appropriation of certain areas
of the hotel by groups which then became identified
with those areas. Attendance at certain events was
also important. Jewish Friday night services were
held each Friday in the chapel, a Protestant service held about once a week in the Theatre Room,
and there were buses to take Roman Catholics to
Mass each Sunday, as well as an occasional Mass at
the hotel. Regular or even occasional attendance
at one of the religious services would establish a
resident as a "member" of that small group. Those
who attended the religious services were largely
those in circles 3 and 4 reality participation
circles, although there were some circle 1 and 2
people. If a new resident was seen once at a
service he would be asked on other occasions: "Will
you be at the Friday night service today?" or "Which
Mass are you going to this Sunday?" Therefore,
if he continued to attend, this aspect would be
incorporated into his hotel "identity" and he might
then be described as: "A nice person, active in the
Protestant group." Others would use this information in interpreting his actions. For example, if
this same man was seen to push a woman out of the
way so that he could get on the elevator first,
the two following interpretations among others
could be made. (1) "I just don't understand it, he
goes to church every week and seems like a nice
man. Maybe he got some bad news and was upset. (2)
"I'm not surprised. A lot of those fellows are
hypocrites--go to church all the time and hate
their fellow men. Me, I never go to church but I
try to be as kind to others as I can."

Thus, by simply appearing at some events, an
individual can establish himself, in the eyes of
others, and in his own eyes too, as a participant in

one sort of shared reality. Of course, the interpretation of this reality will differ slightly from
person to person and group to group.

A new resident can establish himself in the
eyes of others as a fairly lively person simply by
coming to all planned events and taking an interest
in them, even if he contributes little. If he is
not seen at any events, he will be considered to have
no interest in social life, and it may well be months
before more than a few people are aware of his existence. If a person establishes himself as an isolate,
notice will be taken of his activities while alone
so as to "place" him. For example, if he is seen
to leave the building purposefully each day, he
will be thought to be lively, and if he hangs about
the hall staring, he will be thought to be "out of
it."

Presence at classes or lectures creates some
sense of community among those with like interests.
If a class is being given there will be certain
people who can be counted upon to be there. This
is so much the case that class members will check to
see if the right (i.e., expected) people are there
at the beginning of each new class. Remarks such
as the following will then be heard: "Oh! Where's
Thelma Henderson? I know she would be interested
in this. She wouldn't want to miss it. She must
have forgotten. I'm going to go ring her room and
remind her." Thus, when a resident establishes
himself as being interested in certain things, he
is expected to maintain that interest and to maintain contact with the group which shares those
interests.

Two other non-conversational means of creating
and maintaining a shared reality at Mayfair were
dress and demeanor. Taken together these two
aspects could almost allow a Mayfair resident to
place another resident correctly in the reality
participation circle in which he was involved. This
is all the more interesting as there is a fairly
restrictive dress code imposed upon the residents
by the management. The code was designed to insure
a pleasant atmosphere at Mayfair and avoid a "nursing home" look. Men are required to wear a tie at
all times--a rule which is quite strictly enforced,
but continually disputed--especially in summer.
Women were supposed to wear stockings at all times
and to be "appropriately dressed." At the begin-

86

ning of the research period a bulletin was distributed regarding the proper wearing of pants by women
residents. The pants could be worn if they were
part of "a co-ordinated pants outfit." The elements
of the outfil should be harmonious as to color and
style, and one element of the outfit should be "a
jacket or tunic which covers the hips." It did not
seem that the women objected to these dress instruc-
tions nearly as much as the men objected to wearing
a tie. Not one woman listed the dress code among the
things she didn't like about Mayfair House, while
about 75% of the men interviewed found the rule
about ties to be a nuisance.

Even within the guidelines of the dress code
there is room for tremendous variation. There were
residents who were immaculate and fashionably dressed,
and some who, tie or no tie, looked as if they had
just gotten out of bed. Attention to clothes is
characteristic of the groups interested in social
life--either within the hotel or outside the hotel.
The liveliest volunteer at the local hospitals was
a woman who was extremely interested in clothes.
She had a large collection of beads and earrings,
and never appeared without jewelry co-ordinated to
her outfit. A brown dress would be accessorized
with gold, a blue one with blue necklace and earrings in a lighter but matching shade, pearls
would appear with a black dress, etc. It was fun
to see what she would be wearing, and it was obviously a source of fun for her as well. Certain
other residents always appeared dressed in quiet
good taste. One woman was known for her collection
of cheerful, colorful pants suits.

On the other hand, clothes were a means of
expressing "out of it-ness." A woman known as an
eccentric expressed herself further with her rather
wild choice of hair bows. Large bows in bright
colors appeared atop her hairdo. Several people
said: "Just look at that! Wouldn't you know she'd
be the one to do a crazy thing like that?" Perhaps if someone else had worn such bows it would
have been ignored or even accepted, but in combination with her known eccentricity, it was just considered to be further evidence of her strangeness.
Another woman wore dresses which looked like house-
coats. They were actually dresses and the management could do nothing about it, but she looked as
if she had just stepped out of a bath. In fact, she

was not much involved in what went on around her, and her way of dressing emphasized this fact.

Dress could also be misleading, although it usually gave correct clues as to the reality participation circle of the individual. One man was so well dressed and purposeful looking when the research began that there was some questions as to whether he was a resident or visitor. Conversation with him later showed a man with almost no interest at all in what was going on around him, either in the hotel or in the world. He had lived at the hotel for six years. He wanted to go over his achievements--real and imagined--of the past. As the research went on, the man appeared to be more and more slovenly, but his dress still suggested more involvement with other people than he displayed.

Another resident, who was removed from Mayfair House after what was interpreted as psychotic behavior, was also very well dressed and had at first given the impression of being very much in control of everything. A staff member said the morning that this resident had been removed from the premises for violent behavior: "I couldn't believe it! When he first moved in here I went to greet him and I couldn't find him because he looked so young and well dressed that I thought he was just visiting someone here. He always looked so nice! How could we ever know what was going to happen?" Everyone, even staff, was using dress to determine something about the residents' inner state.

In most cases, some conclusions could be correctly drawn from dress. A woman who came to Mayfair at an early age after an illness was quarrelsome, depressed in manner, and very untidy. As weeks passed and she began to find herself more at home, her manner and her dress began to improve. She began to wear jewelry and to go on shopping expeditions. She bought a few new clothes in brighter colors and took an interest in having her hair done and her fingernails painted. Compliments from staff and other residents seemed to give her confidence and she became more pleasant. She began to take an interest in the running of the hotel and to go out to the theatre and on other excursions. All of these developments took place almost simultaneously, and of course, the change in dress was only one element. However, it was the most visible element, and in this case, did indicate a change in her general reality circle participation.

Some of the residents were well aware of the impression which their dress produced upon others. A very sick woman who was growing steadily weaker continued, until the day that she was taken to the hospital for the last time, to dress with precision and style. She was a dominating personality and refused to give up that role until the last. When she died it was discovered that she had been very poor, but no one knew it from her way of dressing. She had worn good shoes and good suits with suitable jewelry. No matter how ill she was, her hair was beautifully in place. She had always looked to be very much on top of the world, and she had worked very hard to produce this impression.

Part of the importance of demeanor is the association of a certain person with a certain type of activity. We have mentioned the woman who worked on the switchboard and the gift shop earlier. As a rule she was involved in one or the other of these two activities when anyone saw her. Therefore, the impression she produced was one of a very lively person. Her demeanor was an attentive one, and she was actually a good observer of what went on around her. She was rarely seen doing nothing and this is one of the requirements of being considered lively. Others tend to define a person's reality participation in terms of what the person is usually doing when people see him. Therefore, a person who is seen day after day standing in the hall doing nothing is considered to "out of it" and someone who is sitting everyday in the Greenhill Lounge is said to "one of the gossips," and a person who goes to all the meetings and participates in discussion is "active."

This brings us to the important idea of being busy. One could almost draw a line between the one and two reality participation circle people on the one hand, and the reality participation circle 3 and 4 people on the other. The difference here would be that the circle 3 and 4 people always appear to be busy and the circle 1 and 2 people do not. The circle 3 and 4 people will sit on the patio in summer and enjoy the warmth and the flowers, but they will not be found anywhere inside the building in the public rooms unless they are doing, or are about to do something specific. [2] These people are people who have something to do and define their reality very much in terms of what they do. Therefore, it would be detrimental to their feelings about themselves and to their relationships with other busy people to be seen doing nothing. They do not sleep in the public rooms, but rather do their reading, thinking, and sleeping in their own rooms.

Whether or not one appears to be busy is an important aspect of general demeanor upon which people are judged acutely. Work, or the appearance of work, was important. Kleemeier (1951,1954) shows that the possibility of working in age adds to the well-being of the retired person. Some of the residents who were lively and involved in many activities had the knack of appearing (or perhaps they actually were!) exhausted by all of their many activities, so that if they flopped down to rest in the card room, they implied by words or just actions that they were sitting there because they were tired from all of the many things they had been doing. One woman did this. She would sink into a chair near a group of others and say: "Whew! It's too much! I don't know how long I can go on like this with so little help. I work this place--for free! And when I work everyone enjoys the good results. But I'm tired. I'm too tired to go up to my room. I'm just going to sit here for a while." Thus, she was justified in her own mind for sitting as long as she liked without being one of the "passive ones." In fact, she did do a great deal or work especially towards the production of the monthly newsletter, and she did not want this to be un-noticed.

Actually, in the social groups of Mayfair, as in the society at large, a great deal of positive value was attached to "doing something" as opposed to being really retired. In fact, the advertising campaign of the hotel makes it clear that they hope that all residents will be active and will contribute to making the life of the hotel more interesting and making their own lives grow and change. This is the rhetoric of the hotel, but in actuality, only a portion of the residents have the health, drive, or even the desire to make an effort to be busy--even though all may affirm that activity is "good." Many of the residents formerly had the sort of job in which all activities were laid out

by the foreman or "boss." Unless they are unusual
people, they find it difficult, late in life, to
become highly self-motivated. In retirement they
often are at a loss and do not know what they want
to do. If the hotel activities do not appeal to
them, it takes a great deal of motivation and energy
to find something else to do to keep active. If
poor health is a problem, withdrawal from other
people and planned activities is more likely.

Individuals who were previously involved in
club and club-like activities found it much easier
to "find something to do" at Mayfair. Three Social
Directors at Mayfair remarked that the ones who
took part in the activities and committees were
women, and that it was hard to involve many of
the men. Discussions with the active women indicated that almost 100% of them had been involved
in clubs and committees before they retired. Many
of the men who had worked at jobs involving manual
labor said that they had never had much time for
clubs before they retired, and preferred to be "independent" of them after they retired. Clubs and
committee work simply were not their idea of "doing
something," and since these activities were the main
thing to do at Mayfair, people who felt this way
often ended by "doing nothing" in terms of the social
groups. Thus, there were more men than women at
Mayfair who were "doing nothing." This tended to
contribute to the prestige of the few men who were
active in the hotel life and outside the hotel. They
contrasted sharply with other members of their sex
and were in good position for occupying the few
leadership roles available.

There is a wide range in the types of demeanor
which can be observed at Mayfair, and a wide range
in the sorts of busyness in which the residents can
involve themselves. Those involved in circles 3 and
4 reality participation found it necessary to have
the demeanor of solid, involved citizens who had
something to do each day. They created the reality
of their type of involvement with the world through
conversations with others who could affirm this type
of reality, through participation at certain events,
and through maintaining a certain level of control
over elements of their environment. Some of the
circle 3 and 4 people emerge as leaders and this
role further affirms their reality participation
circle membership.

In any social group, leadership has to do with power, and, as we shall discuss later, one of the problems of leadership among the residents at Mayfair was the small amount of power to be distributed among the few leaders. In the absence of power, backed up by meaningful sanctions, cynicism may prohibit the emergence of really capable leaders. This is very much the case at Mayfair, where the main types of power sought was simply the power over one's own life, and power to influence others, power which few could hope to attain.

However, there were things at Mayfair which needed to be managed and people were needed to manage them. Although every committee had a staff "sponsor," a chairman from the residents had to be elected. Things often fell into disrepair and it was necessary for some of the residents to speak to the staff about it. Some of the residents needed help in managing certain aspects of their lives, and staff had no time for this. It was in these areas that the resident leaders were needed and, in fact, did emerge. Although it seemed that the resident leaders were acting as assistants to staff, they were actually looked up to by most of the other residents; they themselves felt that they were performing a useful function. These leaders were sometimes called "too bossy," but most people appreciated what they were doing.

The question of the emergence of leaders was considered over many months of observing at all committee meetings and watching the general social life of the hotel. It became clear that, once an individual was established as a leader, he or she was likely to maintain his or her position unchallenged for a long time. One man was elected to be chairman of a certain committee for about the tenth year running. It was very hard for the livelier people to get rid of their elected offices once they tired of them because few willing and competent replacements were available. The resident leaders did much work and kept the committees going even when some of them, such as the Dining Room Committee, were only for show and effected minimal changes.

The staff encouraged the leaders a great deal, for they were the example of what everyone at Mayfair House should be like. The only problem was that there would not have been enough committees to head if everyone had wanted to be a leader. From time to time, new groups began, but it was difficult to get people to be involved with new projects. Also, staff expected, and got, support for their own projects and ideas from the leaders who were able to "see their point of view." Resident leaders were listened to more carefully than were other residents by staff and some were called upon to "explain things" to their fellow residents. Thus, the more capable and willing residents became rather unofficial staff members--feeling that they had a definite job to do and trying to do it regularly.

Just as conversation was the means of defining shared reality, so it is the means through which leaders emerge at Mayfair House. There are no silent leaders. The best place for an individual to be noticed is at the committee meetings where it is encouraged for newcomers to speak as long as they don't speak too much. Doing volunteer work was the quickest way of receiving recognition, because there are never enough people to visit hospitals, help others to the clinics, do errands for those less capable, etc. However, conversation with the people of the volunteer committee, as well as good works, is a quicker way to recognition.

Another way to a leadership position is to have a good eye for the problems of the building and a quick tongue for describing them to other residents and staff members. Noticing repairs which need to be made and telling about them puts one in a good position morally, and one is apt to be asked about other things as well. A new resident who complained about litter on the patio was listened to carefully at a Hotel Maintenance Committee meeting. She was asked to be sure to mention anything else she noticed at the next meeting. If she then brought another legitimate complaint to the next meeting and continue to attend the meetings, she would probably eventually be elected as chairman, vice-chairman, or secretary.

Because there were few people who were willing to be leaders who work but have little power to change things, there are usually opportunities for new leaders to emerge if there are people who want these positions. It might be well, at this point, to clarify exactly what we can understand by the word "leader" in the context of Mayfair House. As we have said before, leadership in any context, usually refers to power and control and use of sanctions. The power and control and sanctions are exercised over people and over things. At Mayfair House the question of control over things is absurd, for each resident controls only his own belongings and shares the rest of the hotel with the other residents. As has been pointed out, groups can, through usage, appropriate certain rooms which are public, although they can never prohibit "outsiders" from using them. No individual ever appropriated an area for himself, although the woman who ran the gift shop came the closest to making the gift shop "her" area. She did succeed insofar as people who did not like her felt uncomfortable in the gift shop and would try to make their purchases when she was not there.

Socially sanctioned control over other people, as an aspect of leadership, was weak at Mayfair House as well. There were very few sanctions which an individual could exercise over another. Gossip or reporting someone to the staff were the two ways most often used by residents to try to control the behavior of other residents. These methods were only successful if the individual reported was involved with other people to the extent that talk or a reprimand from staff would be meaningful to him. There were residents who would not have noticed if people were talking about them and who would have immediately forgotten any reprimand by staff. There was one man who offended people constantly by spitting on the floor. Every time he did so a staff member would be called and would go to him and reprimand him sharply about it. He would always say he was sorry very pleasantly and promise never to do it again. He always forgot and did it again.

To return to the question of control over people, it cannot be said that any of the Mayfair leaders actually had much control over the actions of any of their fellow residents. Rather, they had a certain degree of control over the climate of opinion among those residents who were involved in reality participation circles 2,3, and 4. They may have even had some control over the circle 1 people whom they knew personally. This control over opinion gave them power in the sense that they were respected by other residents, and perhaps more importantly, they were respected by the staff. Many residents would "go along" with the opinion of a resident whom they considered to be a leader. Therefore, the leaders were important to the staff in helping to put across rules (such as only ten people to an elevator at one time) or new ideas (such as a weekly discussion session with the main Administrator). The staff are the people who are running the hotel and because they make the rules they have actual power over the residents. They could ask someone to leave the hotel and they are the ones who selected the new residents. Residents are aware of the power of the staff and they tend to respect those whom the staff respected. Leaders had respect from the staff for their position as opinion influencers, and they were deputized as additional staff members. The leaders themselves were aware of this and their attitude to staff was distinctly different from that of many of the other residents. Leaders felt that the staff would be unable to function without them and that they (the staff) often did not know what was going on. A woman who did various small jobs for the main Administrator, and who also led some committees said: "That man! He's really nice but he's so disorganized He doesn't know what he's doing half the time. He wants to do this and that for Mayfair House, but he doesn't know how he's going to do it or where the money is going to come from." She felt that she was helping him a great deal (and, in fact, was) by telling him what was possible in the context of Mayfair customs and budget.

The resident leaders are also aware that they are in a better position than staff for knowing all that was going on among the residents. They knew if there was someone who was becoming too senile to find his own room at night, and if there was someone putting garbage outside his room in the hall. This sort of information was vital for the staff to know in order to evaluate the state of the hotel at any given time. It is also the sort of information that it would be hard for them to get without watchful people who would come and tell them. In this way resident leaders who identified their interests with those of the staff and who would act as sources of information, were invaluable. Therefore, they were treated with respect by staff, and often given extra privileges.

Considering all of these factors, it is possible to make the following statements about leaders at Mayfair House. (1) Leaders act as sources of information for staff and residents; (2) leaders act as mediators between staff and residents; (3) leaders participate in planned activities, and tend to be active directors of the ones in which they participate; and (4) leaders are mainly involved with reality participation circles 3 and 4, and are strongly engaged in maintaining the circle of reality with which they are involved, as the main one of the shared life world.

This leads to more points concerning achieving and maintaining a leadership position. First of all, it is not every resident who is interested in being a leader. As we have mentioned above, there were certain positions on committees, etc., which had to be filled by residents. The surest way to being noticed, an important factor in becoming an opinion influencer, is to take active part in committees and other planned activities. Not all residents are interested in participating in these activities,but they are the only real entree to the role of resident leaders, for through the committees one is brought into contact with staff, who are the real holders of power in this life world. Therefore, the role of leader is confined to those people who are willing to take an interest in the affairs of the hotel. There were quite a few lively people operating in circle 4 reality participation who were not, and would never be, leaders because they refused to take part in the hotel activities. Either they considered them "small time" or too boring to bother with. These individuals could perhaps have contributed a great deal to the social life of the hotel, but something drove them to seek amusement and fulfillment elsewhere. Other individuals, also interested in the world outside the hotel, make the world inside the hotel one of their interests as well, and were very active in all aspects of hotel social life. These people and the circle 3 reality participation people are the groups from which leaders were drawn.

The beginnings of leadership lie in the active participation in the hotel committees, where interested people are most welcome. After an individual has established himself as a person of consequence, he can safely drop some of his committee work, but he must appear in public frequently and must frequently give an opinion on things. One man who had established quite a following of people who "went to him" for help with all of their problems from love life to income tax, went to very few meet-

ings. He had already become so well established that
people came to him without his having to make many
public appearances. Nevertheless, he did appear
if there were any important meetings and he always
came to hear any important speaker, always asking
questions after the talk. He participated in few
committees, but he never allowed himself to become
invisible. He also went to some pains to make sure
that any new residents came to know him and to appre-
ciate him and his role. A woman said during her
second week at Mayfair: "Mr. X came up to me the other
day in the card room while I was reading a letter.
He introduced himself and said that I should come
and ask him if I have any problems. I told him
that I usually ask my niece, but he said that she's
not always around and that he is always there to help
people." In fact, during the research, Mr. X became
suspicious that his functions were being usurped
because so many people were sitting in our office
talking. He took care to come in himself to assure
himself that what we were doing was different from
what he was doing. Once he felt reassured, he was
very friendly. Mr. X. is an example of the long-
time leader who has almost cut off all contacts
with the committees which originally afforded him
the opportunity to be noticed.

Actually, most of the resident leaders maintained an active interest in committee work and, as
we have remarked, it was almost impossible to recruit
others to replace them. There are not enough people
who are interested and capable, as well as being
willing to accept leadership positions which are
actually so poor in potential for bringing about
change. It was certainly not impossible for resident
leaders to engineer some changes in their lives,
and in the hotel life, but these were rather minimal.

Once having established oneself as a resident
leader, it was normally not difficult to maintain
that position, although there were challenges from
time to time, and one must continue always to be
"seen." Challenges were rare because most of the
residents were delighted to have someone else run the
committees. Once in a while, however, an individual
tries to challenge the particular "clique" which is
running a committee. In the spring of 1975 a group
was in charge of the Dining Room Committee. This
group was determined to see and to speak about only
the good things in the dining room and meals. In

meetings, one after another, they rose to speak about
the loveliness of the decorations for Easter, the
nice fried chicken, the good ice cream, etc. If
there was a complaint, a compliment came first to
soften it. These were all very pleasant women, so
they insisted on a picture of the dining room that
was perhaps too rosy. A new resident came into one
of these meetings and spoke: "I thought the beef
we had last night was terrible. I could hardly chew
it. Another woman at my table was given a piece
that was all fat. Finally she got two bites of tough
meat. I also object to the overcooked vegetables.
They look grey and unappetizing." Some of the members of the committee looked as if she had just ex-
ploded a bomb. Obviously she didn't know the rules
or she would have sugarcoated this pill. The food
services director responded in a very surly way and
another woman then spoke saying that "any kitchen
can make mistakes" and "we all know how hard our
food staff work to make things as nice as possible
for us." Until a much later time, the woman who
had spoken in a manner so different from the pre-
vailing mood in that committee, would have no
chance to become an important member. Later, if
things changed and the "nothing but compliments"
group broke up, she might have a chance. Being so
out of tune with the group running the committee
would prevent her from having an important role at
present. At the end of the research the optimistic
group was still in charge of the Dining Room
Committee.

The most important element in maintaining leadership is simply to remain on the scene and to keep
making comments about everything--to be very verbal.
If a resident does this, there is very little chance
that he will lose his position as a leader in the
minds of all of the other residents. If a leader
is troubled with bad health this can be a real problem. Most of the constant leaders were rather robust people, although one of the most prominent
woman leaders spent some time in the hospital and
had to have a quiet convalescence after her return.
The saddest thing which happened during the research
was observing the attempts of a very sick former
leader to retain her position as a leader when she
was failing both mentally and physically. She was
totally unfit for any of her former activities,
and yet she persisted in trying to take part, creating a painful spectacle for everyone. Actually,

only death or total disability can really disqualify a leader, once he or she has established a position.

Leaders, then, are important at Mayfair House mainly in terms of their roles managing committees, helping others, and in maintaining a shared reality. Most of the people at the hotel look to leaders for affirmation of reality as they experience it. As we have said, leaders operate mainly in circles 3 and 4, but there are also important circle 2 gossip group leaders. These leaders are not as universally recognized by the staff, or by the circle 3 and 4 residents, but they are definitely important as opinion leaders. Often these individuals are the source of rumors, both true and untrue, which circulate at Mayfair House.

Turning to the more "visible" circle 3 and 4 leaders, we can see that they, in cooperation with staff, try to maintain a community reality, and a practical and "realistic" orientation to people and events. A cheerful view of things is encouraged, and these people lead a valiant fight against the depression which awareness of the all too real problems of illness, poverty, and loneliness can bring to residents. The reality which the circle 3 and 4 leaders try to stress is one of optimism and continuing possibilities, even though cynicism and discouragement do creep in from time to time. This reality is very attractive, and those who "believe" in it are very acceptable to their fellow residents as leaders. Helping to present this type of world as the true one, and doing the busy work of the committees give the Mayfair leaders full-time jobs. Those who are willing to do the work of the committees and who, by example, give an acceptable picture of life in retirement are valued leaders because they keep up the spirits of their fellow residents and take the initiative in maintaining a tolerable world view.

Footnotes to Chapter VI

1. This response is similar to that termed "armored" by Reichard, Livosn, and Petersen (1962). The "armored" type of response to old age was one in which the old person, not wanting to be passive or face the idea of decline, kept himself very active.

2. The idea of "active retirement" embraced by the hotel staff was also accepted as a positive value by almost all of the residents. Almost without exception, the people who said they liked living at Mayfair House were busy with hotel activities a large proportion of the time. The people who ex-ressed the most dissatisfaction were the isolates who were not senile, but were very aware of the aloneness.

CHAPTER VII

THE LIFE WORLD: KEEPING IT STABLE

The reality which the staff of Mayfair and the resident leaders wish to protect is the reality of a normal cheerful community involved in numerous shared experiences. Activity, new experiences, and growth are assumed to be part of this reality. Like all systems of assumptions, this reality is constantly challenged by occurrences which seem to disprove it and which must be systematically fought. In <u>The Sacred Canopy</u> (1969), Berger says, speaking of the religious world view:

> The world of sacred order, by virtue of being an ongoing human production, is ongoing confronted with the disorganizing forces of human existence in time. The precariousness of such world is revealed each time men forget or doubt the reality-defining affirmations, each time they dream reality-denying dreams of "madness" and most importantly, each time they consciously encounter death. Every human society is, in the last resort, men banded together in the face of death (1969:52).

In the sense in which he speaks, all images of reality are religious in the setting up of a cosmological order and of images of truth which, if they are challenged, leave man rather comfortless. At Mayfair, the system of reality which was acceptable to the staff and to the residents was actually supported by the religious beliefs of most individuals, but could also be taken up with no religious commitment at all.

It would be extremely difficult, if not impossible to describe in detail all of the elements of the most widely accepted view of reality at Mayfair, but it is possible to outline some of the main assumptions. These are not unique to Mayfair House, but are the most strongly stressed values here. The

main assumptions which were seen to be most strongly
protected by the Mayfair residents are as follows:
(1) Life is precious and has meaning; (2) life is
best lived in sharing experiences with other people;
(3) as long as one lives there are possibilities
for change and development; and (4) individual action
can be effective and it is meaningful. A person will
get out of life what he puts into it.

Of course, there are hundreds of other assumptions
and half-assumptions which go into the view of reality sketched above, all of which give variety to the
life world. Each individual has a slightly different
version of it, but the four ideas listed can be said
to form a very loose basis for a world view which
many of the Mayfair residents tried very hard to
maintain. Basically it is this world view which
staff and resident leaders work to protect from
events, ideas, and people who could destroy it. [1]

There are constant threats to the maintenance
of this frail world view and the threats are very
strong. In the months at Mayfair, however, 4 threats
were repeatedly fought by both staff and residents,
and appeared to be the most common ones. They are
as follows: (1) Rebels--individuals who strongly
presented conflicting world views; (2) irresponsible
people--mentally deficient or senile people; as
well as chronic alcoholics; (3) poverty--the fact
that many of the residents were terribly poor brought
into question the ideas that change was possible and
that a person could be individually effective; and
finally, (4) illness and death--the ultimate threats
to all levels of reality participation.

We shall consider each type of threat more fully
after outlining the most commonly used methods of com-
bating all four. Naturally, death is a special case
and must be seen as a threat on the most basic level.
It is dealt with differently depending upon whose
death it was, where it occurred, whether it was expected, etc. In all other instances, threats to the
maintenance of the desired reality are met in the
following way at Mayfair: (1) By active aggression
against the offender if it is a person. This aggression may take the form of gossip about a person;
(2) by ignoring or discounting the threat if it is
a person, a condition (such as poverty) or an occur-
rence (such as a death); and (3) by physically re-
moving the threat--usually this means staff action

to move out an irresponsible, rebellious, or very
ill resident.

Rebels have a hard life at Mayfair. They are
usually lonely, and they are subjected to very ag-
gressive behavior on the part of some of the other
residents. Two rebels come to mind immediately, both
of them very strong personalities. One of them is
Emma Throckmorton whom we mentioned earlier as the
eccentric who kept birds flying free in her room
and who wore unusual hair bows. Far from being completely out of it, she displayed, at times, unusual
powers of observation and perception. During a
meeting of the Dining Room Committee she raised her
hand and said to the food director in a thoughtful
voice: "I wonder how much of this you are listening
to. You say you are listening, but I think we're
all just here making fools of ourselves. Nothing
will change because of what we say." In contrast
to the cheerful myth of the effectiveness of that
committee, Emma had spoken a terrible heresy. No
one answered her, and the remarks heard later had
to do with her birds, her style of dressing, and
rumors about her 90-year-old boy friend. The
threatening truth which she had mentioned was not
discussed. Rather, it was necessary to establish
her "weirdness" so that all that she said could
then be safely discounted. 2 In another meeting
which was described second-hand, Emma had apparently
had enough and said that she did not think committees of old people were worth anything and that
this was because no one wanted to hear what old
people said, so it didn't matter if Mayfair had a
delegation to an elderly peoples' convention which
was to be held in the area. These remarks came
out of her own cynicism, her own experience of
poverty and powerlessness, and her inability to be
optimistic and pretend that things are a bit
better than they really are. Although these remarks
may have echoed the doubts of others, she was met
with hostility because of them. Moreover, by all
accounts, she nearly came to blows with another
woman because of them. The scene ended with Emma
stomping out of the meeting followed by remarks of
"crazy old thing" and gossip about how she had tried
to move her boy friend into her room, but the staff
would not allow it. Emma was unable to maintain a
"social self" and insisted on intruding her own personal and threatening views into situations which
depended upon a certain amount of pretense. There

was a great deal of gossip about her, and some ostra-
cism although the second meeting described is the only
instance of a direct personal attack on her. Rather,
she was regarded as a source of fun by some residents,
and pitied by the kinder ones for her loneliness. She
was always in trouble with staff because of her practice of keeping food for the birds in her room. This
food also brought cockroaches, which made her unpopular with staff and with her near neighbors. Because of her extraordinary lucidity and sarcasm on
some occasions, she was not a "harmless" eccentric,
but a rather threatening one, and thus, she was
met with aggression, rather than simply being ignored.

Another rebel is Jack Stein. He is a very independent person who has had a dislike of institutions
all of his life. He sees Mayfair House as an institution, like a jail or a hospital and speaks of it
in this way. He says that he lives at Mayfair out
of economic necessity, but looks down upon the other
people who live there, assuming that they have chosen
to live in an institution and thus have no sense. He
often fails to consider that others may have come to
Mayfair for the same reasons that he did. [3] He loudly
deplores all aspects of life at Mayfair to anyone
who will listen, making him rather unpopular with
staff. He tells a story of a staff member half his
age who reprimanded him in public for not wearing
a tie. He later went to this staff member's office
and "told him off" in no uncertain terms for his lack
of courtesy and tact. He gives this example as proof
that people who live in institutions are not respected as real people. His stories make residents very
uncomfortable because, as exaggerated as they are,
they contain elements of truth. His forthright manner, obvious clarity of mind, and the absence of any
markedly "peculiar" traits make him a very dangerous
rebel. Some of the resident leaders have taken a
dislike to him and consider him a "troublemaker,"
telling others to avoid him. However, his strength
of personality and clear mind make it difficult to
combat him. He was not the victim of any successful
gossip, as he kept his private life to himself and
any false rumors were so ridiculous that few took
them seriously. One of his strong points was that
he never pretended to be anyone he was not. He
would say: "These people here are nobodies. I'm not
anyone special either, but you don't see me pretend-
ing that I used to be a big shot and I still am.

These people are nobodies and they always were, but
they try to make you think that they come from good
families. Yeech, some of them are as low as you can
get and I tell them that to their faces!" Obviously
this was not the way to popularity. Jack was ostracized more than anything else. He was known to be
"difficult" and, in talking with new residents, he
usually imparted this information himself. He would
say to a new person: "They will tell you not to talk
to me, and they will say that I am a dangerous person, so if you want to speak to me you had better
be ready for that." He was lonely but at times
rather proud that the other residents actually worrie
about what he would say. He was, perhaps the strong-
est and most successful rebel at Mayfair, and he knew
it. This gave him some satisfaction, but he said
he was very lonely and would have loved to find someone that he could have talked with successfully.

Poverty among some of the residents was another
threat to the maintenance of a positive world view
and belief in the possibility of a happy and fulfilling retirement. 4 There were a number of individuals
who, after paying the monthly rent which covered
their room and meals, had no more than a few dollars
as pocket money. One woman, whose case several
people were working to improve, had nothing at all
left after paying for her room and meals. She had t
depend on relatives for things like toilet paper and
personal necessities. She had no close relatives,
so this put her in a very precarious position.
Other residents sometimes gave her clothes, but hers
was a very bleak existence.

No one at Mayfair was in danger of starving.
Many residents had lived there for months without
paying their rent with constant, but not harsh reminders from the Administrator. An Administrator
said: "We would never really throw anyone out if the
lived here for a long time, if they get into financi
problems and can't pay their rent for a few months."
It was their policy to "carry" quite a few non-payer
because a large proportion of residents did pay thei
rent and paid on time. The type of poverty of which
we are speaking here is not a question of life and
death of the physical being. It is a question of
life with dignity and possibility. If a person
cannot even buy small necessities for himself or
herself, the possibilities are very limited. He or
she cannot leave Mayfair for an occasional meal, and

he or she cannot go on excursions which require money,
no matter how little. They cannot contemplate moving, and they cannot afford a change of scene from
time to time. In a society where economic power is
primary, a person in this financial state cannot help
but feel that they are simply not a part of the outside world because they cannot participate in the
activities of the outside which require an outlay
of money.

To a person of any age, to be poor in the midst
of a society which has many prosperous members can
be a devastating experience. It can lead to depression, cynicism, and above all to a feeling of utter
powerlessness. When this is added to the other
problems of an aged person, the combination can be
debilitating. This problem, faced by many at Mayfair,
gives the lie to the rhetoric about "the freedom of
retirement." There are many satisfying things to do
which require little money, and yet, a minimal amount
of free cash for small expenses is really necessary
for self-respect and for allowing the individual to
arrange new experiences for himself. Often families
of residents fail to understand this when they accept
the idea that at Mayfair "everything is provided."
Bringing the elderly parent or grandparent a monthly
bag of candy, toothpaste, and toilet paper does not
solve the problem of his feeling economically helpless, even though there is a room to sleep in, and
a dining room to eat in, and clothes to put on. In
this society, money represents possibilities of all
kinds. Without money, an individual feels locked in,
and not part of the society outside Mayfair. Some
residents conceal their poverty so well that no one
knows that they are in a bad way. No one wants to be
pitied, so resodents usually keep their money problems
to themselves. No one wants others to be saying of
him or her: "Poor thing, he/she has nothing, maybe
I should offer some of my old clothes." Everyone
at Mayfair wants everyone else to think that they
are "doing all right" and some of the residents on
public aid were very anxious that their fellow residents should not know this. Many were quite willing that "outsiders" should know that they were on
public aid, but would say: "Please don't say anything to any of the people here about it. They are
so nosey and want to know everyone else's business."
So, this was one of the problems which got in the
way of the beautiful "picture" of the reality of retirement at Mayfair House. Of course, starvation was

not a problem, but the presence of poverty was distinctly unnerving, therefore, the way the problem
was usually dealt with was by ignoring it. No one
wanted to talk about their own financial problems,
although speculation about other peoples' was interesting. No one wanted to think that some of their
fellow residents were "really poor." Many had worked
hard all of their lives, and found it a real disgrace
to be old and not to have a penny to show for it.
It is a bitter problem which was systematically
swept under the rug.

Another threat to the maintenance of a pleasant
reality at Mayfair was the presence of what we have
called "irresponsible" people. These are the senile,
mentally deficient, or alcoholic residents. Theo-
retically, as Mayfair is a hotel for "well" residents
who can take care of themselves, there should be very
few people of this type in residence. Actually,
there were quite a few, and their presence and its
attendant problems is profounding disturbing to
the other residents. Their presence evokes a kind
of fear in the others, a feeling that all is not well
and that perhaps the promises of the hotel advertising campaign are not true. Above all, these individuals brought up questions such as: "Could this
ever happen to me?" "Has this happened to me and I
just don't realize it? and "Why am I here if this
is a place for people in that condition?" There was
an overwhelming desire not to identify with these
people, a frantic attempt to disassociate oneself
and all one's activities from them. It was almost
as if these unfortunates could communicate their
unhappy conditions like a disease to anyone who came
too close to them. Speaking of proper conduct at
social gatherings, and social gatherings as an
expression of the larger social life in which they
are imbedded, Goffman discusses the discomfort which
a group feels when someone conducts himself in a
bizarre manner:

> Aside, then from the disrespect an individual
> shows to a gathering by conducting himself
> improperly, such improprieties can also cause
> the others present to fear for their physical
> and social inviolability, whether rightly or
> not" (1963:197).

It is the social "inviolability" which is the most
feared for at Mayfair. As we have described, the
community is fragmented into various smaller groups

held together mainly by the similarity of the reality participation circles of the members. These groups (except for some of the circle 1 people), together with the staff of Mayfair, act in cooperation to create a reality which is close to the reality of the participation circles of the various groups, and acceptable in a larger sense--that is, it can be presented to the world outside as the reality of Mayfair. Irresponsible individuals who could be expected to do something bizarre at any moment were a serious threat because, not only could they shake the image of reality which residents were trying to hold, but they could give outsiders a very peculiar picture of the world of Mayfair. Obviously, none of the more active and involved residents could bear the thought that a visitor might think that the hotel was populated by only irresponsible and unaware old people.

One day there were quite a few people in the lobby waiting for the elevator. Then, staggering through the main doors came one of the chronically drunk residents. He walked unsteadily toward the elevator with the obvious intention of trying to make it up to his room. The small crowd dissolved like melting snow. Some went to use the back elevator, some decided not to go upstairs and disappeared, some simply moved away from the elevator and stared at the man. Suddenly, he fell flat on his back. No one came near him, but from a distance, someone called: "Call someone! Look what he's done! It's disgusting!" When we were trying to help the man to his feet, only one resident came to help. I drafted one of the hotel's cleaning boys to help get the ill and incoherent man up to his room. One woman resident came along, speaking to him quite kindly: "You'll be up in your room soon. Why did you have to go and drink so much? You're going to kill yourself. You should be more careful!" She was the only one who appeared to notice the incident in any terms except "Isn't it disgusting. Get him out of the lobby!" etc.

The response of the woman who spoke to the drunk and went along to see that he got to his room was the unusual one. The common response of residents to months of almost daily incidents of this sort was one of first expressing disgust and hostility towards the person and then ignoring the whole thing. Another woman had a problem of alcoholism. She appeared entirely unaware of what was going on around her when she had been drinking, and when she was sober she was not very aware either, only afraid. Over the months her behavior was very strange. She would appear in the dining room with no shoes, unable to find her table. She fell down several times in the dining room and once she was found by the police walking down the middle of a very busy street, oblivious to the dangers around her. Everyone commented on this woman's behavior and said, "She ought to be in a hospital." In fact, there was talk of getting her into a hospital for her alcoholism. There was a strong desire on the part of the residents to get her out of the hotel. It was impossible to ignore her behavior because it happened so often, and it was clear that she was unaware of the hostility that she was generating because of her actions. It was settled with the Administrator that she would go to a hospital "soon." As it happened, the problem was solved in a very sad way. After an evening of drinking she fell in the hall of the hotel near her room, hit her head on a pipe, and died. Her next door neighbor found the body and was immediately in a very agitated state. Apparently she had felt so hostile and angry toward this woman for the disturb-- ances she made while drunk that she had wished her dead more than once. Finding her dead outside her room, she was stricken with conscience. She said: "I didn't really want anything like this to happen. I just wanted them to take her away to a hospital and dry her out." Others said, "Isn't it sad!" and were obviously terribly relieved that it had happened. The general relief felt at the death of this woman is indicative of the hostile feelings and worry which her presence at various events had caused. She was almost invariably disruptive. Gossip and personal attacks could not touch her. She was somewhat aware of being ostracized, but was really too withdrawn to react to it at all.

We have already spoken of the man who stood in the hall all day. He spoke to almost no one and simply stared at passers by. He was very inoffensive, and the residents dealt with him by ignoring him altogether. He could not participate in group occasions because he had a speech defect and could not concentrate for any length of time. It became clear the extent to which he was ignored when he disappeared for several days and no one even noticed that he was gone. In fact, it was a part-time staff member who saw that he wasn't standing in the hall and decided

to have his room checked. Then it was clear that he
had not been at home for several days. The Administrator was notified, and after checking around a
bit, the police found him wandering about--several
miles from the hotel. No one knew where he had
been sleeping or if he had eaten. No resident had
even noticed that this man was missing, much less
reported it to the Administrator. Who knows how long
he could have been gone if a staff member hadn't
remembered about him? Socially, at Mayfair, the man
simply did not exist, therefore, when he disappeared
physically there was not too much change in his
status from the point of view of the other residents.
Probably this man should have lived somewhere where
the staff could have spent more time giving him the
minimal social contacts that he needed. As we have
pointed out before, some comversation was necessary
for him and he did seek out staff and others who
would listen to him from time to time. However, his
"blankness" at times was too disconcerting to the
residents to allow him to be included in any of the
social groups whose reality was sustained by conversation.

     Illness and death are the last threat to real-
ity maintenance that we shall discuss. Illness,
being something that everyone must deal with at
times, was rather efficiently handled by most of
the social groups at Mayfair. However, the illness
must be of a physical rather than mental nature.
Mental illness, senility, deep depression, and any
of the manifestations of alcoholism were too disturbing to be "accepted" by the Mayfair residents.
People with these problems had to be ignored, or
treated with a certain amount of hostility. There
was a strong feeling that they should not be living
at Mayfair, and this is probably true, as Mayfair
can offer little of the type of help that such individuals need. Physical problems were everyone's
lot and as such were discussed with much interest
by all.

     People's physical illnesses were rendered
inocuous by much discussion, comparison of what different people "had" and a great deal of conversation
about medications and doctors. In a sense, illness
could be "controlled" by making it a kind of group
possession. Of arthritis, one could say: "Oh yes,
I have it too and I take the extra strength Anacin
for the pain." And another could discuss the merits

of Ben Gay in relieving stiffness, etc. Serious problems like heart attacks and strokes are "shared" in
the same way. Everyone, even if they have been
lucky enough to escape these illnesses themselves,
knows someone who has suffered them and they can
describe the treatment, the recovery period, and the
problems of life after recovery. Far from being
a taboo subject, illness was discussed to the point
where it lost its impact.

Visiting people in the hospital, sending cards to
them, keeping track of who was ill with what was a
social activity participated in by most of the livelier residents. Even the circle 1 reality participation people could occasionally be counted upon to
show an interest in someone else's illness--especial-
ly if it was one they themselves had experienced.
Illness was a topic of conversation which individuals
with different circles of reality participation
could discuss with equal interest. It affects individuals, groups, and the whole of the hotel. There
was so much illness that it had to be dealt with and
incorporated, as it were, into the ongoing life of
the hotel.

Death was another matter. Of course, the impact
of any death at Mayfair was dependent upon a number
of factors. The most important one was how important
to social life at the hotel the person who died had
been, and how well known the person was. Other important matters were questions of whether the person
had died suddenly or had had a long illness, and
the matter of where the death had taken place. Naturally it was more upsetting all round if the person
had died at the hotel rather than at the hospital.
All of these factors were conditioned in their effect by the person's place in the overall scheme of
life at the hotel. We have discussed the case of
the alcoholic woman who died in the hall after a
drinking binge. This was the most upsetting sort
of death--sudden, at the hotel, with the body being
found at the hotel. Yet, few people were very upset
by the incident other than the neighbor who found
her. Her behavior at the hotel had become so upsetting and embarrassing to all that no one felt
much more than relief when the poor woman finally
died. She had not taken part in any of the social
groups so no one really knew her well. She was
known by sight to almost everyone, which made her
more isolated than ever because most people avoided

her. Knowing of her strange behavior when drunk, most people said that they had expected her to have some sort of accident. Therefore, her death was not unexpected and not altogether unwelcome because it solved the problem of what to do with her which had been troubling everyone. These factors acted to "soften" the shocking aspects of her death and to make it not particularly upsetting to most people.

When questioned, the staff said that they "try to keep it quiet" when there has been a death at the hotel, but that somehow almost all of the residents hear about it immediately. Staff said that most deaths are deeply distressing to the large part of the residents. They try to prevent deaths from happening at the hotel by getting sick residents to the hospital as soon as possible, and by not allowing them to return unless they have made quite a good recovery. They try to see that the less promising cases go to nursing homes rather than coming back to Mayfair. Nevertheless, with so many elderly residents, sudden deaths do occur,and the people must develop ways of dealing with the upset feelings that these deaths elicit. Early in the research, after the death of a rather new resident, this conversation was heard: "Did you hear, old Mr. Singer died, just suddenly passed away." Response: "Everyone's got to die sometime. It was just his time. I didn't know him very well, did you?" First speaker: "No, but he seemed all right, not like that damn Smith with all his talk about money. I can't stand that sort, you know--the kind who brag all the time about what they have." Response: "Yeah, I agree. That Gordon is a pain too. All he talks about is how hard he worked in the depression and made a lot of money afterward."

The speakers just touched upon the subject of the death and moved on to other topics. This might seem a rather casual approach, and a bit hard-hearted, but one must remember that these residents had to hear this sort of news much more often than the person who lives in a community with mixed age groups. They had to be able to assimilate the news at a surface level or they would be upset most of the time.

Some deaths were profoundly moving for the majority of the residents. The woman discussed earlier who had fought so desperately not to give up her place in the committees and who tried to have a

hand in all hotel affairs up until the day of her
final departure for the hospital left almost everyone
upset after her death. Even when she was ill and
very unpleasant to everyone she had seemed very much
a presence. She seemed more alive than other people,
and in contrast, also seemed more dead. For several
days people talked about her--how much she had done
in the old days, how she had hated to give up, how
they respected her even if they didn't like her.
They were moved because someone who had been a
moving power in the life of the hotel was gone. The
livelier residents saw themselves in her, and feared
that their own days of activity were numbered. There
was a real feeling of mourning among many people.
A memorial service was held at the hotel for her and
a large number of residents were there. Life wasn't
really "normal" for several days.

On the individual level, a person's reaction to
a death at the hotel is very dependent upon his
reality participation circle. People engaged at
circles 3 and 4 appeared to be more affected by a
death, particularly a death of one of their own
social group's members. These people saw such a
death as a real threat to maintenance of their
reality. They truly felt a loss--to themselves personally and to the group which the deceased had
been a part of. People engaged at circle 2--the small
group, were affected by deaths depending upon how
well they had known the individual who died. Deaths
were a constant source of talk among the small groups,
but they did not appear to upset people operating
at this level as deeply as it did people at circles
3 and 4. Circle 1 people were affected by the death
of another person only insofar as they could themselves identify with that person. If, for example,
the person who died had been seated at their dining
table, or had been someone who helped them to walk to
the clinic each week, the circle 1 individual might
be very upset. If the person who died had had a
similar condition, that might also be upsetting.

It is not surprising that, as in the world outside the hotel, the more an individual was engaged
with life and the activities of life, the more disturbing his death was likely to be. There was a
feeling that death was appropriate for some individuals, but not for others. When a resident had
withdrawn from social activities and was living within his own thoughts and memories, there was a feeling

that he or she was not really there anyway. The
person had removed himself, so to speak, and death
was only a natural continuation of the removal pro
cess. This is the sort of social disengagement discussed by Havighurst, Neugarten, and Tobin (1968:161),
decreased interaction with others, and an increased
preoccupation with self. In the article, Cummings
and Henry's (1963) controversial and questionable
view of this process as a natural, even desirable one
is discussed. It allows a person to leave the world
by stages, rather than abruptly. Another view which
may be advanced is that of the older person trying
to maintain his social world as long as possible and
being forced to relinquish meaningful contacts
(Neugarten 1961:161). At Mayfair House one could
find both types of elderly people--those who were
engaged with the world at many levels until death,
and those who withdrew from all the activities of
the world and for whom death seemed only a small
step more. Whether a process of "disengagement"
took place seemed to be a matter of individual health
and personality. What was clear, however, was that
disengagement by an individual prepared others for
his death, and made it seem less a shock than if he
were fully involved with the world one day and dead
the next. It is also clear that the residents most
involved with the world, with 3 and 4 reality participation circles, were the most shocked and upset
by any death. They were the least willing to accept
death--probably because they felt that they still
had a great deal to do in life.

There is no really successful way for residents
to deal with death as a threat to reality maintenance.
There is no way for any group to lessen the solemn
impact it must have upon them. But, as we have seen,
all deaths, though disturbing, were not equally disturbing and some deaths did little to disturb the
round of daily life. At Mayfair, people learned to
protect themselves from too much pain, by not involving themselves with any death too much unless it was
it was so close to them, or the death of such a significant resident that they could not ignore it. The
only way to deal with death was to see it as "appropriate" and expectable for some individuals and to
try to overcome shock in activity when death came
suddenly and unexpectedly.

Even the most disengaged residents usually could
not contemplate their own deaths calmly. One day
one of the most withdrawn, although fairly lucid

114

residents, came to the office. She came in and asked
that the door be shut. Obviously agitated she said:
"I went to Mr. Schultz (a resident) about this and
he said he'd help me, but he wouldn't. I wanted to
ask what I should do about my funeral arrangements--
how I can pay for them and have the kind of funeral
I want. But he wouldn't even listen. He kept saying
I was going to live for a long time and there was
no need to worry about that now. But I am worried.
I have $400 saved and I'd like to have a Jewish
funeral and I don't know what to do about it."

She said that she had nothing else to spend her
money on and would like to be sure about her arrangements. We contacted a Jewish undertaker for her who
said that they often made arrangements ahead of time
and that he would be glad to send someone to the hotel
to talk with the lady. She seemed pleased, and a
date was set up. Some days later we received a call
from the funeral director who said that when the
representative had called at Mayfair, the woman had
said she knew nothing about the planned visit and
that she "felt good" and would not be making any
funeral arrangements for a long time. She had obviously not forgotten, as she came and mentioned
the matter to us. She simply could not face the
business of making funeral arrangements for herself,
even though her conversation was full of statements
such as: "I won't be here much longer, thank God,"
"I'll be glad when my troubles here are over," and
"my life means nothing to me now." She seemed disengaged, but death was too large a step even to think
about seriously.

Active residents and staff alike are all eager
to maintain an atmosphere of a pleasant reality
of a retirement hotel in the face of all of these
threats. It is in combatting these threats that the
most full cooperation between staff and residents
can be found. On certain occasions they can be seen
to almost act as one group. When a present threat
is not seen there are all sorts of tensions and dis-
agreements between residents and staff and there are
complaints of "they never consider what we want"
from the residents. However, maintaining an acceptable reality is in the interests of both groups and
when there is a real threat, Mayfair House will be
very nearly united to combat it.

Footnotes to Chapter VII

1. This presented some real conceptual difficulties, because it was often the case that the type of relations between staff and residents was itself threatening to the maintenance of belief in the four assumptions named. Both staff and residents wanted to believe these ideas, but the fact that the staff were so powerful and often so dictatorial and felt that they had to take so much initiative in engineering social life cast doubt upon the assumptions even while they were being affirmed.

2. Emma had violated the norms of the situation in which she found herself. Goffman (1963) sees every social occasion and its participants as a kind of little society. "Situational proprieties, then, give body to the joint social life sustained by a gathering, and transforms the gathering itself into something akin to a little social group, a social reality in its own right" (1963:196).

3. Jack varied between being an "angry man" and a "self hater" as described by Reichard, Livson, and Petersen (1962). Sometimes he blamed others for his disappointment with life and other times he blamed himself. Usually he assumed that everyone, including himself deserved what he got. He would say: "I can't stand this place. I don't like the people. I don't even like myself. I never did anything right."

4. The reality of poverty for many old people is beyond dispute (see the Introduction). Additional information and suggestions for improving the situation can be found in the 1974-1975 Report of the Special Committee on Aging, United States Senate.

CHAPTER VIII

STAFF AND RESIDENT LEADERS: UNEASY ALLIES

The staff are primary in importance at Mayfair
House, both as leaders in protecting a shared reality against threats and in possession of actual power. As we have discussed earlier, a certain amount
of hypocrisy is involved in the relations between
staff and residents. In theory, the staff are
there to make the hotel run smoothly and to make
life pleasant for the residents. In fact, they
think of themselves as managing the hotel as an
institution, and they are thought of by many of the
residents as the "bosses." [1] One staff member's
response to a heated discussion by residents during one meeting was "Aren't they precious?" indi-
cating that he took none of what had gone on very
seriously. Some of the more thoughtful residents
seriously objected to this attitude, feeling that,
because they were residents, everything they had to
say was classified as being unimportant.

There is a certain amount of frustration in the
feelings of some of the residents toward the staff
who are many years younger than they are. One
woman became exasperated with the social director
and lashed out at her: "You can't understand the
problems of old people. You are young and haven't
even seen life yet. You aren't married and you
have no children. How can you know what it's like
for us? They should get an older woman who knows
something about life." No answer could be made to
this tirade, because it was true. One of the liveliest men said of a new young administrator: "He's
not a bad person, but he's young and doesn't know
the first thing about this job. He thinks he
knows all about it, but he has a lot to learn."

The anger and frustration come in when the youth and inexperience of some of the staff are contrasted with the very real power which they exercise over the lives of the residents, many of whom could not move even if they wished to do so. It is hard to be told to wear a tie by a woman young enough to be your granddaughter. It is the staff to whom a resident must come with important problems such as incompatible table mates, problems in their rooms, committee problems, etc. A staff member is part of every committee and most meetings. They are the ones to whom resident's relatives talk to find out "How Grandpa is doing?" and they are the ones who decide whether one is too sick or senile to continue to stay at Mayfair. Being considered "helpful" by staff can make an individual important at Mayfair and being considered "a nuisance" can make his life difficult, for little attention will be paid to his requests.

All of the important decisions at Mayfair are made by staff even though they may be influenced by pressure from residents. As we have pointed out, there are too few staff members to do all that should be done for the residents in terms of service. It may be added that perhaps staff concern themselves where they are not needed at times,-such as in committees. However, it has become a commonplace expectation at Mayfair that staff is always "busy." This means that they are almost always too busy to sit and listen to one's problems. Staff has made "busyness" a kind of status symbol at Mayfair, contrasting their overwork with the leisure of residents in a rather self-righteous way. Activity is, in the context of Mayfair House, a sign of importance. Staff members accentuate, and perhaps exaggerate their own activities to stress their own importance and to deflect any new involvements from themselves. The Social Director was heard to say constantly: "Oh, what a day I'm having. There's the newsletter to do, and then our guest speaker, and I'm having some trouble about Mrs. Sawyer's table, and we have two new residents coming in today. Please, don't bring me any new problems." She also had the habit of moving about the building at a kind of half-run. This accented the effect of being very busy and also prevented any residents stopping her for long and perhaps inconsequential conversations. No one who was not either very fast or very loud could stop her before she had passed by.

Their frenzied activity and extensive contacts with the outside world give the staff superior status as reality protectors, for it is their sort of reality participation circle which is most similar to the residents' level 4 circle. The outside world is considered by most of the residents to be the "real" world even though they might spend most of their time and thought in far smaller, more particular worlds. The level 3 and 4 residents are the leaders and their perceptions of reality are shared by the staff to a large extent, and thus are lent extra prestige. Staff and leaders together produce through constant dialogue, two versions of the reality of Mayfair House. The first version is the one which they themselves believe is the true picture, while the second is a further idealized version which they wish to present to the outside world. The official "real" picture is an idealization of life at Mayfair and the "active retirement" while the "guest" version is just a prettier idealization. Staff and resident leaders have reached a tacit agreement both about what is real and about what should be presented to strangers as real.

The difference between these two pictures is appreciable, but not huge. There is no real wish to deceive the public, rather a desire to present the best side of things when there are strangers present. This is somewhat the same as the slight differences in family behavior when guests are present and when the family is alone. The "public" side of life at Mayfair is thought to be a true picture--only without any negative elements.

To return to the matter of complicity in maintenance of reality by resident leaders and staff, a kind of hierarchy of residents, ranked according to their "helpfulness" (this may also be translated as "co-operative in maintaining the order which the staff would like to see maintained") exists in the minds of the staff. They have mental lists, communicated to one another, and under constant revision, of who among the residents can be counted on to help make social occasions go, smooth over difficulties, and who can make a good impression on guests. These are the people who embody the characteristics which staff would like to see in all residents. They are depended upon by staff every day and they are not unaware of their importance. A long-time leader and powerful personality said, when asked if he ever went to the administrator with problems: "No, he comes to me with problems. He's new and he really doesn't know who's who and what's what around here. I go into his office fairly often and tell him what's going on." This was probably a true analysis of the situation, although the administrator, if asked, would most likely have said that he was just having a friendly chat with the man and not have admitted that it was a briefing session.

Different staff members have different roles in the business of reality maintenance at Mayfair. The head administrator is the first representative of Mayfair House, as far as the world outside is concerned, but he actually has far less to do with the residents than does the assistant administrator and the social director. The problems that he deals with are mainly administrative ones, and mechanical ones, such as seeing that the building is properly maintained. He is usually only involved in major social problems of the residents, as in the case of deciding whether to ask someone to leave because of alcoholism or senility. Some of the really active resident leaders do talk with him regularly about a number of problems, but the average resident leaves him alone.

The lack of dialogue between the administrator and a large number of the residents was recognized, because a weekly talk session was established. At this session the administrator usually made a short presentation about some problem or topic which he wished the residents to think about. This was followed by an open session during which any resident could bring up any topic which he wished to discuss. Some of the meetings turned into bitter complaint sessions because people saved all of their grievances to present to the administrator at once. Sometimes this included complaints against the other residents and more than once quarrels between residents broke out and the administrator acted as a referee. Sometimes, the more tolerant residents grew impatient with the complainers and told them what they thought and this also made for more quarrels. Reflecting upon the always tense air of this meeting it began to be plain that there were so many quarrels because the residents were frustrated by the lack of contact between themselves and the administrator. He was seen as an inaccessible "power"

as most residents had been conditioned not to
"bother" him when he was in his office. When he was
actually there, available for talk, all sorts of
old quarrels, and seemingly irrelevant problems came
to the surface because he was considered the top
"boss" and therefore, the final arbitrator. Everyone's problems seemed to erupt at once. After each
of these meetings some of the residents would express amazement at the irritation and excitement
of some of the others, at the tension, and the
anger. These meetings were difficult for the administrator, too, and very often they were concelled
without notice if he was "too busy."

The Assistant Administrator and the Social
Director were actually in much closer contact with
the residents and were much more involved in the
cooperative business of reality maintenance. The
Assistant Administrator is officially supposed to
deal with rentals, but he is involved more with the
small individual problems of the residents. He is
the one to whom they go if a social security check
does not arrive, or if there is a money problem.
He is the one who assures the residents that problems can be solved, although he is himself subject
to depressed moods because he does not always believe it. He jokes a great deal with the residents
and sometimes will even joke about their problems,
trying to make them seem less serious. His presentation of the "guest view" of the reality of Mayfair
is not very convincing, probably because he is involved in so many serious problems and because he
really cares about the residents. He is more tem-
permental than the Administrator, but is also
seen by the residents as "more human." Some of them
dislike him intensely, but no one ever said of him
that he was "a fake" or "didn't care" as was so often
said of almost all the other staff members.

The Social Director is the person most intimate-
ly involved with reality maintenance. Being in
charge of all aspects of the planned social life,
with the entertainment of guests, and the super-
vision of outings, this is natural. She is constantly juggling the "guest" and "everyday" realities of Mayfair and trying to keep any other unacceptable realities from raising their heads. This
puts her in the strange position of trying to tell
people what they should be thinking. She is in
charge of dining room seating and often has had to

be the peacemaker at table quarrels. She often says
something like this of people: "Now Mrs. Green, I'm
willing to change your table, but you might not like
the next one any better. I know you get tired of
hearing the same stories day after day from Mr.
Martin, but there are a lot of other people here
who tell the same stories more than once. I know
you are a tolerant lady and you can understand other
people's problems, so please think about it and tell
me later if you really want to change your table. We
all have to put up with our friends' peculiarities,
don't we?"

In a meeting where she was sponsor, she might
say: "Everyone! That's not the way we solve things
at Mayfair! We don't quarrel--we discuss things,
and we let everyone have a chance to have his say.
Please stop this shouting and let's discuss this as
we should." In the dining room when the daily announcements were made, some of the residents would
go on talking and the Social Director often said:
"Excuse me, but I can't talk when there are so many
other people talking in here. We all know that it
isn't polite to talk when someone else is speaking.
Even if you aren't interested in what I'm saying,
someone else at your table might be, so let's all be
quiet and listen."

She was constantly reminding people of how things
"should be," holding up the "guest" picture of reality at Mayfair as the ideal toward which people
should strive. She was the one who spent the most
time with the hotel corporation's Public Relations
Director and she was well aware of the importance
of creating an image in dealing with the public,
and in maintaining an image for the residents themselves. Her job is a tense one, because she must
constantly watch for things which "spoil the picture,"
and she must take steps to correct them. All three
of the Social Directors who were at Mayfair during
the research, tried, to a certain extent, to avoid
too much contact with the residents. This was
usually done by being too busy to be involved in
many things. In some sense it is understandable.
It is difficult enough to be the main protector of
the acceptable reality of Mayfair without having too
many reminders of events and people who do not fit
this image. Actually she could function best, in
this role, having minimal contacts with any of the
residents other than the leaders who would support

the image of acceptable reality. In fact, only the resident leaders, or other individuals with very strong personalities did have extensive contact with any of the Social Directors.

In spite of the youth of all three of the Social Directors, they functioned in very much the same way- as a kind of casual mother to the residents. They planned events and brought in entertainment, but they did not take a really active part in anything that was going on unless there was some sort of trouble. They would break up any quarrels, and tried to solve dining room seating problems. They tried to keep social events going in a successful way, but they never actually joined in any event as a participant. One felt that they were there but not there at the same time. They maintained a real psychic distance from everything that was happening except when they had to intervene personally and to exercise authority to get some situation resolved.

One Social Director said the week before she left: "It was really getting to me! You see so much and there are so many things you can't do anything about. My nerves can just take so much. I love these people, but I feel dragged out. They take so much out of you. I've got to get into work with a younger livelier group." The work of the Social Director is not hard, but it is the strain of trying to be always optimistic, energetic, and appearing to believe that retirement at Mayfair is wonderful which is exhausting. The Social Directors, although all were cheerful women, had a tendency to be vaguely irritable much of the time. They had an air of being "put upon," and a slight touch of martyrdom about their busyness. This irritability was im- perfectly covered by a synthetic cheerfulness which fooled no one. These people were doing the best job that they could. They were simply placed in a false position by the requirements of their job.

As we have said, the Director of Food Services is the one staff member who displays her superior power openly, and does little to maintain the idea that the hotel is run for the pleasure of the re- sidents. Unlike the Administrator, Assistant Ad- ministrator, and the Social Director, she does not feel that her job has public relations aspects. Actually, she is less visible, as her job does not require that she attend any social events or meet any guests or prospective residents. Nevertheless,

her open enjoyment of power, and her obvious oblivi-
ousness to what residents think, is a disturbing note.
She does not help to maintain the acceptable reality
for the residents. Rather, from time to time, her
behavior suggests another, very unacceptable reality.
It suggests the reality of lack of choice and helplessness which is so often a part of old age. It
suggests that older people should do as they are
told or something bad could happen to them. 2

The good will of the Food Services Director is
important, for, if someone misses a meal, she can
see that he gets a place at the next sitting, gets
something to eat at an odd time, or gets nothing
at all. As has been pointed out, she can serve
or withhold the favorite foods, such as watermelon
and fruit pie. She is the one who decides if someone has a legitimate complaint or not if he sends
back a plate of tough meat. No one talks about it,
but everyone knows that it is a bad thing to be
considered a pest by the Food Services Director.

The following dialogue took place at a meeting
of the Dining Room Committee:

Mrs. Green: Yesterday at dinner I was given a piece
               of meat that was all fat, and I asked
               one of the waitresses, Martha, to get
               me another plate. She came and looked
               at it and refused to get me another.

Mrs. Food
Service: Had you eaten any of the meat?

Mrs. Green: Well, I must have tasted it to see how
               bad it was, but I ate very little. The
               point is, she was rude to me, and I was
               left with no dinner.

Mrs. F.S.:   I just want to get to the bottom of this!
               George (her assistant), you go back to
               kitchen and get Martha. I want to know
               what is going on.

(George went out and returned in a few minutes with
 Martha who looks very worried. She is Mexican and
 speaks very little English.)

Mrs. F.S.:   Martha, Mrs. Green, here, says you were
               rude to her and refused to get her a

<pre>
                    new piece of meat at dinner the other
                    night.

Martha: Yes. . . .I remember, but she had eaten
                    all of the meat when she asked for more.
                    You told us not to give second helpings.
                    That's why I said no.

Mrs. F.S.:   You didn't tell us that you had already
                    eaten the first piece of meat, Mrs.Green.

Mrs. Green: (very nervous now) I didn't eat it all.
                    There was nothing to eat. I just tasted
                    it. That's all.

Mrs. F.S.:   You just tasted so much that there was
                    nothing left! My kitchen can't afford
                    to give everyone two entrees! I think
                    it's serious when my staff are ac-
                    cused too. This was very upsetting for
                    Martha.

(At this point two or three ladies get up and say
 that they think that Martha is a very good waitress
 and that the food is fine.)

Mrs. F.S.:   Martha, you can go back to the kitchen
                    now. I think we are all straightened
                    out now! People! Please realize that
                    I would love to give you all seconds on
                    everything, but I just can't. I have
                    a limited budget, and you all know
                    what food prices are. Please don't
                    ask my staff to do what they have strict
                    orders not to do--to give extras. You
                    are putting them in a bad position when
                    you ask. They do the best they can, so
                    don't make their life any harder!

(Mrs. Green has now been characterized as not only
 greedy but inconsiderate. She makes one last at-
 tempt to save face.)

Mrs. Green: I did not receive a full helping of
                    meat. It was all fat and I only tasted
                    it! Martha was rude to me. I hardly
                    eat anything anyway, and when I don't
                    have any meat I get weak.

Mrs. F.S.:   Now, you can all see what happens when
</pre>

we don't think of the other person's point of view. Martha couldn't give Mrs. Green another helping of meat when the first one was all gone. It was against my rules, and I'm strict about my rules. These girls know nothing when they come to me. I train them completely in my methods. One of the most important things they have to learn is that we can only allow one serving per person. If something is really bad, don't eat it! Give it to a waitress and they will take it to George or me to see. Then you can have a new plate. But I think that's enough on that subject. I want to bring up the problem of people who sit at tables long before it's time for the meal to be served.

Mrs. Green: I don't think this is fair.

Mrs. F.S.: I'm sorry Mrs. Green. We just can't give you two entrees, and now please let's drop the subject.

Mrs. Green is well on the way to being considered a pest by the Food Services Director who went to some pains in this instance to make her look bad. In the future, it will be hard for Mrs. Green to have any problem seriously considered by the Food Services Director, and other residents on the committee will come to share her (Mrs. Food Service's)views in order to keep peace with her. Mrs. Green's best course in the future would be to placate the Food Services Director with many compliments and hope that she will build up enough good will to carry her over any future events which she will want to mention.

The Food Services Director does not have a role in maintaining any reality either guest or everyday. The closest she comes to this is when she puts on a special dinner, such as "Spanish night" or when an anniversary or wedding party is scheduled. On these occasions she takes part--with a show of great benevolence--enjoying seeing the people enjoy their food. Major holidays like Christmas, Easter, and Passover are marked with decorations in the dining room and special meals. Even the minor holdiays like St. Patrick's Day and George Washington's

birthday are marked with decorations and different
foods. These treats are her contribution to creating
the cheerful air that is so much part of the desired
reality for Mayfair. The contributions she makes to
creating a pleasant reality are material, not a matter of what she says or how she acts. As we have
shown, her actions are a denial of some of the feelings which other staff members are trying to build
up in the residents--feelings of autonomy, activity,
growth, and change. Every time she speaks residents
are aware of how much of the pleasure which they
may take in food depends on decisions that she makes.
She wants residents to be aware of her power. She
is a contradictory figure. On one hand the treats
that she plans add zest to life for the residents.
On the other hand, her dominating personality, and
tendency to "put down" residents make her rather
negative as a maintainer of acceptable reality. Resident leaders have relatively little to do with
her because they cannot depend upon what she will
say or do. It is with the other staff members
that the leaders cooperate to build a reality which
they all can accept.

As we have said, the staff consider some of
the residents to be helpful--usually the livelier
resident leaders engaged in circles 3 and 4 reality participation. This includes both the formal
leaders lke the presidents of the committees, the
people who work in the gift shop, and those who take
some initiative in providing entertainment such as
running movies, showing slides, or getting people
they know to come and give lectures, and more informal leaders who have strong enough personalities to
influence opinion. All of the residents who are
"helpful" at least give outward evidence of supporting staff policies and believing in the collective
cheerful view of reality which the staff want to be
general at Mayfair. These leaders, formal and informal, give every evidence of being busy. Like
the staff, they don't have an extra moment in the
day. Staff give positive reinforcement to these
leaders. They will make remarks like this: "Mrs.
Tuttle is a marvel! She knows everything that's going on, and she's so active--President of one committee and secretary of another! She's 80, but
she has more energy than I do. She also keeps an
eye on everything around the place, and lets us
know if something is wrong. I don't know what we'd
do without her!" These remarks will be made over

and over again--often in Mrs. Tuttle's presence.
Thus, Mrs. Tuttle is encouraged to "keep up the good
work" and other residents are informed both of the
kind of attitude the staff like, and of Mrs.
Tuttle's favored position with them.

What are the ways in which helpful residents
are helpful? As we have said, they are a sort of
deputy staff member, and actually do some of the
work of the staff. To outline more fully the ways
of helping, it must be made clear that everything
that a staff member does could be done by a resident,
if they had the energy and authority to do it. Cooperative retirement facilities run by residents
with a few minor employees for such things as food
service and building maintenance are a real possibility for the future. Giving information, doing
the work of committees, helping with less capable
residents, and living the picture of successful retirement are the main ways in which the resident
leaders help the staff. They can also be depended
upon to be available when visitors come so that
they can be "shown" as the ideal types of retired
people. When a well known television actor who
plays the part of an older man in a very popular
program came to entertain at Mayfair, the Social
Director made sure that one of the resident leaders,
a man well over 80 years old, had many photographs
taken with the famous visitor. These were to be
used in public relations later, and to be displayed
at Mayfair House as well. In the Social Director's
office there was a large display of photographs of
well known personalities who had come to speak or
perform at Mayfair. Usually some residents were
pictured with them. It is interesting to note that
the same residents appear in picture after picture.
These people are the resident leaders, the ones the
staff consider helpful. They are recognized by
the staff, complimented, given these and other small
privileges, and, what is even more important, they
are likely to be listened to when they speak. Other
residents know this and will often go to a resident
leader with a problem--hoping that he will then
take the problem to a staff member who will give
it more attention than if they had approached the
staff member themselves. These small privileges
set the leaders apart from the other residents and
give them slightly more control over their lives
than the others.

Cooperation in creating and maintaining a
shared acceptable reality with staff is the main
way in which most of the resident leaders are helpful. In order to do this they must be very sensitive
to the public relations image of Mayfair, the "true"
but optimistic picture which the livelier residents
share, and other less desirable "true" pictures
which the facts and problems of old age constantly
intrude upon the scene. They must believe in the
possibility of a happy and productive life after
retirement strongly enough to suppress, in themselves
and others, any suggestion that something else might
be true. Many very clear-minded residents were not
leaders simply because they were unable to pretend
to believe this picture. A strong woman, Mrs.
Keebler said: "You know, they tell you that these
are the best years of your life because you have
time to do things. I don't agree, Almost everyone
I loved is dead now. When I was young, I worked
hard. I had a husband and four children who needed
me. I didn't have a moment to myself, but _that_ was
happiness, _that_ was living. Now I have all the
time in the world, but the people I loved are gone.
Who needs all that time! When I was young I was
happy, not now!" Mrs. Keebler did not believe any
of the Mayfair rhetoric, therefore, she could not
project a sense of believing a really "happy" picture of retirement hotel living. She would not
be a leader because she really did not feel that all
of the activities involved in being a leader were
worthwhile.

The resident leaders do believe in an optimistic
sort of truth about Mayfair, although all may be depressed from time to time. Their lives involve
enough interaction with a variety of other people
to keep them in touch with different viewpoints,
and to make the world seem interesting. They are
aware of the need for recruitment of new residents
for Mayfair House, and they are most anxious that
the sort of people who move in should be people
like themselves. It has been often said in this way:
"It's really important to get the right sort of
people here. We want people who will add something,
you know? Not people who will be a drag on us all.
So we have to _be_ the right sort of place--give a
good impression--or the kind of people we want will
go somewhere else and we'll get all the duds."

The creation of a good impression for outsiders

who may be a source of new residents is a very important point to both staff and resident leaders. The
resident leaders can become furious at other residents who act senile or "nutty" in front of outsiders. Perpetuation of the hotel as a distinct
social unit depends upon the constant recruitment
of new members. These new members will determine
the type of social interaction and will create the
image of reality for the Mayfair residents of the
future. Therefore, it is important that lively, interested, and able people should want to move into
Mayfair. Both resident leaders and staff are very
much "on parade" when an individual comes to make
inquiries about Mayfair as a possible home for himself or for a relative. The visitor is shown all
of the public rooms (perhaps omitting the Greenhill
Lounge) and perhaps a few empty apartments to give
him a sense of the place. He is shown all of the
advertising booklets and some of the residents who
are dependable will be called in to "tell him all
about life at Mayfair." The Social Director escorts
the visitor around choosing people to talk to--ap-
parently at random. Actually, she is very careful
who gets to speak to a visitor.

Sometimes all of these strategies go wrong and
something very funny can happen. During the summer
months a relative of the corporation's president
was acting as Social Director during the vacation
of the regular Social Director. Some of the residents did not know her, and did not know that she
was the temporary Social Director. Also, she did
not know the residents and did not know who could
be depended upon to help her with prospective residents. One very warm day in August a woman and
her elderly mother came to investigate the possibilities of life at Mayfair for the mother. Following
the usual procedure, the temporary Social Director
escorted the visitors from room to room. Upon
reaching the Billiard Room she though she would
engage a resident or two in conversation. Not
knowing anyone, she approached Jack Stein, a great
rebel and hater of all institutions. Assuming that
he knew who she was, she said: "Hello. How are you
today? We'd like to hear something about the way
of life here at Mayfair." Jack didn't know she was
the Social Director, so he simply answered honestly
(from his point of view): "It's fine if you like
being in jail with a lot of dumb people. This place
is full of a lot of nobodies, and the food here will

make you sick if you aren't sick to begin with. I
think they try to give us bad food so we'll get
weaker and weaker and not give them any trouble."

The Social Director got the women out of there
fast--after telling Jack who she was. He was surprised, although not really repentant. He said:
"Gee, I don't know who the heck she was. She just
came up and asked me what I thought, so I told her.
If she had known who I was she never would have asked me. If I had known she was Social Director I
might not have said so much, but I couldn't have
told a bunch of lies. . . .But I didn't have to go
so far. . . say so much. . . . I guess she's really
mad now!"

It was a case of a staff member not knowing
who her helpers were and not knowing who the rebels
were so she could avoid them in a situation in which
she wished to control the impression an outsider was
receiving. An incident like this where everything
goes wrong points up the many times when nothing
goes wrong because staff and helper residents cooperate to create a beautiful impression. Most of
the time there is close cooperation on these occasions,
because both staff and resident stand to gain if
"desirable" residents are attracted.

To a lesser extent, staff and helpful resident
leaders cooperate to create an idealized picture
of life at Mayfair when relatives come, and certainly when entertainers or speakers come. What a resident leader of great intelligence said about this
was: "Life here is not bad. There are a few of us
who have kept up with things and are living in the
real world. When some one visits, we feel that this
is our home. We want it to represent those of us
who really do things here. We really feel bad when
someone does something that makes the whole place
seem like a home for silly old people. So, we
try to make visitors see the good things about our
life. There's no need to display the problems we
have here." Without exception, this was more or
less the point of view of every resident leader,
although they were not all so explicit. Another man,
not really a leader said: "When my daughter comes
here to see me, I try to be cheerful, and I always
hope that none of the nuts here will act up. It's
not a perfect life, but she's got problems too, so
why should I add to them. I try to make her visits

a nice occasion."

Staff, too, try to make things pleasant for visiting families. They give extra attention to the resident who is being visited--showing that he or she is especially cherished. They may say something like: "We just love your mother, Mrs. Carpenter--she adds so much to the place. We couldn't manage without her!" Mother, then, like the man who is quoted above, makes an effort to seem happier than she is, and introduces her daughter only to the more presentable residents. Of course, some residents will complain to their families, but the more active and involved with Mayfair they are, the more likely they are to treat the hotel as their home and to try to show the better side of life there.

Naturally, the impression which parents wish to give their children of life at Mayfair has a great deal to do with how they themselves feel about living there, why they came, etc. Among the residents, many are very careful to say: "I came here on my own choice--no one forced me to come." The worst thing which one resident can say about another is that he or she was "put" into Mayfair against their will. It is a remark which is made about the most difficult residents--implying that their families had to get rid of them. All of the livelier residents are at great pains to show that they are here because they want to be here. This is also where a certain amount of playacting comes in. They want their families to see that they have made the right choice, if they have chosen to come here. If they did not have a choice, they sometimes want to show their children that they are manging fine without them. The woman we discussed earlier who had come to Mayfair because her daughter had "raised" her rent" so high that she couldn't pay it said: "I never write her, but a couple of times I sent the weekly program of activities to her. I don't want her to think I'm sitting around here crying. I'm doing things and I can get along fine without her interference."

The livelier residents all have a great deal of pride in the decisions which they can make. They have always made decisions for themselves, and they hope to continue doing so. There was potential conflict, because the less able residents need and want paternalism. They want to be looked after and would accept even less freedom of choice if they

could feel that someone cared enough to tell them
what to do, and to make sure that they are all right.
As we have said, this task falls to the more able
residents for the most part, rather than to staff.

The shared acceptable reality must also be
maintained when there are no visitors, and it is
here that another area of cooperation between staff
and resident can be found. There are a few residents like Jack Stein who rebel at the types of
reality which they are expected to believe and maintain, some who are too senile to care, and a
few, living in their own worlds, who like the occasional excitement of an occasional uproar. These
people, as well as unavoidable crises and situations,
are the major threat to the world view which the
staff and the resident leaders would like to maintain.
The staff are committed to the reality of the able
and clear-minded resident, as are the residents
who fit this description. The resident leaders
and the staff work in cooperation to try to maintain
order and atmosphere at Mayfair. They are more
successful in the first instance than in the second.
It is not too difficult to control real breaches
of the unwritten behavior code. Someone who spits
in corners will be asked to leave if he does not
give up this habit. A person who appears in the
dining room in pajamas will be repremended, talked
about, and finally asked to leave if his behavior
does not change. Many people are asked to leave
mainly on the recommendation of the resident leaders
who make it their business to know what happens.

It is much more difficult to manage the people
who do nothing so overt, but simply project a sense
of apathy, depression, or vacantness. These people
are the ones who can give the place a "sad" atmosphere. Their air of resignation is a constant
denial of the "active retirement" philosophy of the
staff and resident leaders. There is nothing that
can be done about them. One of the reasons, it would
seem, that more effort was not made to shake up the
sleepy and passive population of the Greenhill Lounge
was that it is a place of concentration of such
people and could be easily avoided by the active residents, and not displayed to visitors. It was a
place where the "sleepers" could be counted upon to
be, and if they were there, they were less likely
to be in other places, spoiling the atmosphere.
Staff and resident leaders alike said of the Greenhil

Lounge: "Isn't it awful. We've tried everything, but can't do a thing about it." Actually, the passive residents had claimed a territory and they were allowed to keep it because they were not wanted elsewhere, and they "contained" themselves within this territory to a large extent.

The close cooperation of staff and some residents on the question of atmosphere was very obvious when a man came in to the Social Director with a sort of obituary he had written about an active resident who had died: "I've written the story, but it's strong stuff and I'm not sure we should put it in the Newsletter. It's kind of sad." In reply, the Social Director said: "I think in this case it _is_ appropriate. She was so active for the house, we _should_ all feel sad. We must have a serious article about her." In this instance, it would have been wrong not to take special note of a death, whereas, in most cases, it was "appropriate" to play it down.

In conclusion, it is possible to say that the staff, with the cooperation of some of the residents take the initiative in defining the reality of Mayfair House. It is essentially a reality circle 3 and 4, stressing involvement in both the affairs of Mayfair and the world outside. One of the most important social events at Mayfair was the removal, after many requests from staff and others, of an old bar sign across the street which was thought to be a neighborhood eyesore. Refreshments were served on the street and children from a nearby school were invited. It was an event which was supposed to show to all, the involvement of Mayfair House with neighborhood beautification.

Residents involved with reality participation circles 1 and 2 are obviously excluded from leadership positions at Mayfair, as they are not likely to become helpers to the staff in supporting a definition of reality different from the one they are living. Some very lively 3 and 4 reality participation circle elect not to become involved with helping the staff because they resent their lack of real power in this role or do not believe the reality which staff want protected. This problem will be discussed in the next chapter. However, there are a good many 3 and 4 reality participation circle people who do wish to be involved, and they are invaluable to the staff for the real help they provide both in "creating atmosphere" and in helping to keep less capable residents "in line." They are rewarded for their efforts by special regard from staff, by being "busy," and by the feeling that they are helping to make their environment what they want it to be.

Footnotes to Chapter VIII

1. Goffman (1961) describes a more extreme but similar type of ambiguity in the role of staff in the "total institution" such as the prison or mental hospital. "Those members of staff who are in continuous contact with inmates may feel that they, too, are being set a contradictory task, having to coerce inmates into obedience while at the same time giving the impression that humane standards are being maintained and the rational goals of the of the institution realized" (1961:92).

2. A great deal of her power was "no-power" (Korda 1975:13407). She took the moral position of saying no to requests about changes in the food on grounds that she had to keep within her budget, presenting herself as thrifty and reasonable in contrast to the childish and unrealistic residents.

CHAPTER IX

LEADERS WITHOUT POWER

Power deriving from control over material assets is not an important factor in the society of Mayfair House. Most of the residents are not well off, and money and goods are not significant in determining one's place in the social hierarchy. Two other factors are important as types of power. They are, as we have already stated, power over oneself and power to influence other people and events.[1] These are the available sorts of power which may be avidly sought, steadily pursued or given up as lost by various residents. Insofar as social structure at Mayfair is ideational, E. R. Leach's description of social structure as "a set of ideas about the distribution of power between persons or groups of persons" (1954:4) is appropriate to the situation there. People were constantly discussing the distribution of the two types of available power, and were constantly evaluating other residents in terms of their possession or lack of possession of them. The following conversation is an example:

Mr. Katz: Did you know I keep a car? Yeah, I have it in a garage near here. I like to feel that I can go at any time, so it's worth it to me. Whenever I feel fed up, I just get in the car and go. I couldn't stand it to be cooped up here forever like some of these guys.

Mr. Brown: You're lucky. I don't have a car, but I doubt that I'd use it much if I did. I do so much around here, meetings, helping with the entertainment and so forth--that I don't have time for cruising around. Scott is lucky too. He does a lot here during the week, but goes to his son's with his car on the week ends.

Mr. Katz: I used to do more socially here, but I
              get so discouraged because the staff
              don't really take up our suggestions. I
              began to feel like a fool--trying to do
              some things which never materialized.
              So I just keep to myself and have a
              good time doing the things I like to do.
              I don't get bothered about anything.

Mr. Brown: Well, you're really wrong. We got a lot
              done on the House Maintenance committee
              this year. I got people to go into
              the administrator day after day asking
              about ashtrays for the patio. By God,
              he got so tired of hearing about it
              that we got the ashtrays! That was
              great. Also, we got them to give us
              a few more patio chairs. Everyone says
              our committee was really active this
              year. If no one cares to make the
              trouble this place will really go to
              pieces.

Mr. Katz: It's O.K. if you like hitting your head
              against a stone wall. Sometimes they do
              something, but I don't have the energy
              or the patience that you and Scott have.
              Glad you're doing it though. They get
              away with murder because half the time
              we're too fed up with no action to keep
              fighting.

Mr. Brown: I like doing it. When I see those ash-
              trays on the patio I feel real good.
              After all this is our home!

     The conversation touches on the two important
aspects of power at Mayfair. Mr. Katz values power
over his own time and also having mobility. Mr.
Brown values his ability to influence people and
events, and is willing to suffer some frustration to
accomplish his ends. Both men recognize the difficulties inherent in the situation at Mayfair. The
monopoly of power over what happens by the staff
is the main problem. Each man has met it in a
different way. Mr. Brown is constantly engaged
in a battle of wills--trying to get things done
which he thinks should be done against the double
difficulty of resident inertia and staff concern
with other things. The smallest victory is significant

to him, and he is also appreciated by the other residents because he is using his energy to do things
that they may not have the energy or inclination
to do. Mr. Katz, having become discouraged with the
difficulty of influencing people and events is trying to have complete power over himself and his own
activities. He wants to feel that he is "not bothered" so he has centered his attention upon personal
independence from the social scene. Mr. Brown feels
equally independent, but feels that he can be effective in the hotel's common life, so he continues
to participate. He knows and recognizes that the
resident who participates will be rated higher on
the social scale by his fellow residents. The one
thing that was appreciated by almost all of the Mayfair residents was the fact that these were the individuals who were trying to improve the situation
at the hotel, not becoming discouraged by the often
discouraging lack of results.

While many of the residents were very canny
about the real location of power at Mayfair, there
was a great deal of insincerity among both residents
and staff in talking about it. In action the staff
did little to conceal the true power over the lives
of the residents which they possessed, but they
would not admit it verbally very often. They were
like a dominant group in a feudal society, except
that they did not often admit their dominance except to one another. Most of them, when asked
how they saw their roles at Mayfair, would express
that they considered themselves to be in positions
of service. They would express humanitarian concern
for the elderly and would rarely make any reference
to their managerial functions. Among the residents
the expressed attitudes toward staff ranged from
"they're only employees" to referring to them as
"the authorities." In the time of research it became evident that more residents saw the staff as
"authorities" than as "employees." Some of the
residents who had been at the hotel for many
years and had witnessed the extremely rapid turnover
of staff, felt themselves to be in sympathetic
league with staff who were "doing their best"
against the autocratic corporation which hired and
fired at such a fast rate. They saw with sympathy
that the staff could not really do much without
permission from"higher up" and so they were a little
less impatient with the fact that changes were made
very slowly.

On all levels, from the corporation to the residents, there was some pretense that the hotel was solely "for the residents," although there was some feeling that this was not really true. Frustrated residents would sometimes say: "Why can't they get a better elevator? Isn't this hotel supposed to be for the convenience of old people? Who are they thinking about anyway?" Although, as we have pointed out, there was a great deal of cynical conversation about the hotel being run "just for the money," all residents and some staff seemed to refer occasionally to the ideal picture of the hotel which would be run solely for the good of the old people. All were aware of discrepancies between the ideal and the actual hotels, but there was disagreement as to how far the hotel actually diverged from what it "should be." One of the matters upon which there was a very little frankness was the matter of how much say the residents actually had in determining what went on in the hotel. Actually, the residents were not powerless, but poor in power. They used what power they had to the utmost of their ability.

Some staff would admit to doing most of the planning, but would claim that "we want what they want."[2] Some residents would affirm that they were themselves very effective helping to run the hotel, while others would see the place as a total institution like a jail. In between these two extremes there was a very little true and sober thinking about the allocation of power. People were mainly aware of whether they perceived their lives to be happy or not. Those who were happy were mainly the active people like Mr. Brown who felt that they really could do things, or the less active independent types like Mr. Katz who "did his own thing." During the research period it was observed that all of the important changes at the hotel were made on staff or corporation initiative. The changes brought about by residents' action were minimal in kind or effect.

Nevertheless, the meetings with the administrator in which he constantly affirmed "We want your comments and ideas! This is your home! went on. People continued to attend, and whether they greeted this claim with the later remark that "it was a bunch of hogwash!" or resolved to bring in their ideas to the next meeting, they believed that the "ideal" Mayfair House was one where staff and residents cooperated to make an ideal retirement situation. How or when this situation was to be achieved was not discussed except in wry jokes.

In this situation where there were limited opportunities for the exercise of real power among the residents, what were the criteria for respect among them? Some residents actually did have the respect of their fellows, and it was mainly because they were thought to possess one or both of the two types of power that we have been discussing. In this case the thought created the reality to some extent. If people believed a resident had power they respected that person and gave him or her occasion for influencing opinion. In other words, the respected person was listened to.

Appearing to be helpless gave immediate low social status. Appearing to be independent and active, outside or in the affairs of the hotel gave the beginnings of higher status position.[3] Continual proving that one was active in one of these two ways confirmed it. In the case of the residents who were active in hotel affairs, we have already shown that the approval and support of the staff gave additional bolstering to their status as "helpful" and "important" residents.

Thus, through the months of observation it was obvious that possession of any power at all in this society with its very few positions of power, brought respect to its possessor. All power which the residents had was to a great extent usurped from the staff and corporation, who, although they said that they wanted the residents to do what they themselves wanted to, wanted to lay out the guidelines of what the residents were allowed to want. Independence on the part of residents was achieved in an atmosphere which fostered dependence, therefore respected. Activity not directed by the staff was hard to carry through, therefore respected. Change initiated by the residents was almost unheard of, and therefore, if it was achieved, a triumph. Those residents who achieved a measure of independent action and were counted on for help by the staff were respected. Also, those who had separate lives from the social life of the hotel but who were active and clear-minded were respected. Health and vigor accompanied by a clear mind were always respect ed.

Nevertheless, the fact that most of the available power in the life world of Mayfair House was monopolized by the staff was very discouraging to many residents who refused to deceive themselves as to what the actual situation was. A climate of cynicism and defeat pervaded the thoughts of some residents at all levels of reality participation circles. This climate was the main enemy which had to be fought individually and in groups in order to maintain a cheerful atmosphere.

What are the reasons for such a climate? All of the threats to the shared reality are responsible, plus the added burden of the residents' perception of the real distribution of power in the society in which they will probably spend the rest of their lives. All of the optimism and talk in the world cannot alter the fact that the hotel is, in reality, a business and as such, it will be run as a business and not a utopia. It cannot alter the fact that many of the residents have no alternative to living here. Because of financial or family situations, moving, for most residents, is not a real option. In sum, it all means that in many ways the hotel is more like an institution than like a regular hotel. Possibility of changing the environment appreciably, or the possibility of leaving are not very real possibilities for most of the residents. Most, though not all, residents who discussed this said that they were "here to stay." The fact of being "here to stay" affected people in two different ways. Some felt that it was necessary to "make the best of things" and not complain too much. These statements are based on direct questions asked to 100 residents. Others, feeling that they are "stuck" became cynical and generated the feeling of defeat which sometimes pervaded the atmosphere.[4]

Lack of mobility, combined with lack of effective power in the situation, irritated even the most optimistic of the resident leaders. Apathy was a constant spector which haunted even the most active. Jane Hoover, a committee member and volunteer, who was busy all day long said: "You know, we complain about the people who sit around all day and do nothing, but sometimes I think they are smarter than I am. I try and try to do things, but what we can do is so little. It's just busy work, and we never get anywhere with it. The corporation never

listens to us. Sometimes I think I'd be better
off if I just sat in the lounge and dozed all day.
I'd probably be in better health. As it is I get
so irritated. . . ."

Jane was constantly questioning whether what she
was doing was really more important than sitting
and sleeping because she could rarely see the results of her efforts. Many residents were fully
capable of making the decisions which only staff
were making. As we have mentioned, the presence
of a staff "sponsor" on every committee gave the
impression that staff felt that the residents could
not manage the committees themselves. There were
a number of real functions other than the running
of the gift shop which could have been managed by
the residents, had they been encouraged to do so.

Attitudes which interfere with furthering such
possibilities and maintain a climate of defeat are
ideas that retired people "don't want to bother
with the details of running a hotel," or that "no
one but staff can do it." Also, attitudes among
the residents that their fellow residents are "old
fogies" and "can't do things" are responsible for
peoples' failing to expand their field of influence
at Mayfair. Time after time, any attempt by residents to influence affairs of the hotel in an important way were strongly discouraged by the staff.
The residents who helped them to maintain the hotel
life _in its present form_ were the ones who were
encouraged and given special notice by staff. Other
received constant discouragement until they fell
into line as proper "helpers" or retreated from
the involvement in social life which they had
originally attempted.

This brings us to the fact that non-participation in social life was often a protest against
powerlessness and pretense. As we have pointed out,
there were quite a few very intelligent and lively
people at Mayfair who took little or no part in
social life just because they were not satisfied
with the roles open to them.5 Many of them had
made an attempt to be active in the beginning of
their life at Mayfair but had become discouraged.
Jack Stein, for example, was full of ideas--probably
too many ideas for the situation. He was innovative
and lively. He had been systematically squeezed
out of active social life by the more conservative

leaders and by the staff who found him far too out-
spoken. He became one of the rebels--a kind of symbol of rebellion, in fact. He was seen as someone
who would "say anything," and therefore, he was
very dangerous to social situations in which only
prescribed sorts of things should be said. He was
eternally "out of place" and "out of line." However,
he was accorded a kind of grudging respect for daring
to openly deride certain practices and certain people.
He was thought of as someone who was "getting away
with something," and even envied a bit.

Personally, Jack is unhappy although he enjoys
being a rebel. He longs for communication and is
always starting conversations. He wants to interact with people. He just does not want to be in-
voved with the planned social program, or the "official" social life and he says so. His volubility
as a protestor makes many people uncomfortable, so
they avoid him. He cannot be dismissed as senile
by either staff or residents, so many call him a
"troublemaker." In fact, other residents often seemed to be enjoying quoting the outrageous things
which Jack is supposed to have said. On his side,
he makes it clear that his non-participation in
social life is a protest against being dominated by
staff or by those who help them.

What is the price which Jack or any other
resident must pay if they choose not to participate
in the social life as it is now organized? It is
certain that non-participation exacted a very heavy
toll. Unlike some of the other residents who were
lonely, Jack was aware of this and spoke of it. He
spoke of being lonely and "shut out." He spoke of
feeling that there was no way in which he could have
any control over what went on around him. When
he spoke of things that were planned, he always
said that "they" had done this or that. He had no
sense of sharing decision-making, and neither did
he think that any other resident had a real share
in any important decisions. Often he said:

> They (the staff) don't listen to anybody. They
> get a bunch of these nobodies here and they
> let them think that they are important. They're
> not important. They are puppets and dumb
> nobodies. I could have done that when I came
> here at first because I have the use of my
> brain. But no one tells me what to do. I
> let them know that I want to make up my mind.

> Now they just don't see me. Mr._____turns
> his head away when I walk by. It's because
> they know that I can see what they're doing.

Observing Jack and some of the other non-partici-
pants it looked as if the main burden of the cost of
non-participation was the feeling that one had absolutely no power for bringing about change in the
situation. Jack and some others like him, saw the
sense of power that some of the residents leaders
had as illusory. Nevertheless, they envied the
leaders that feeling. In spite of the superior
power of staff, resident power was not altogether
an illusion. Staff, except for the Food Service
Director, were eager to be liked by the residents.
Lack of power and real frustration unmitigated by
many positive experiences were the main problems
the isolated residents faced and the main reason
for feelings of hostility toward staff.

Actual hostility from some of the staff and
residents, and the loneliness of not being in any
of the social groups were the next most serious con-
sequences of their non-participation. Some of the
isolates did have one or two cronies with whom they
talked occasionally and several, like Jack, were
constantly on the lookout for new people with whom th
can interact.   Nevertheless, they felt excluded,
even though they had chosen their isolation. They
felt resentment and they knew that the only way to
gain even minimal respect in the hotel was to participate in the activities. Jack, and one or two
others were constantly trying to force themselves
to get involved. Jack would go to hear speakers
and then, when there was discussion afterward, becom
enraged by some of the things which the other residents said. He would listen for a while, then
walk out in a temper, looking for someone to tell
what stupid things the "nobodies" had said. He is
intolerant, yet always testing and trying the social
scene.

Jack and others like him are angry that they
could not be allowed to "be themselves" without
being excluded. It is true that the life world of
Mayfair is fragile and too much controversy tends
to destroy the agreed upon veils of illusion which
staff and residents alike wish to throw over certain hard facts of their situation. As in all other
social situations, the conventions agreed upon

facilitate daily life. Jack's "frankness" was extremely unwelcome and as we have noted, he is too
vigorous to be dismissed as senile. Certain other
residents who "said things" were simply ignored
and the hostility directed toward them was minimal.
Jack wanted social life, but he did not want to compromise to the extent that compromise is required
in this situation. Discussing his past life with
him, this is not surprising. He would tell many
stories of how he lived life on his own terms and
"got away with it." Although he was always law
abiding, he seems to have a lifelong disdain for
some of the more petty aspects of social interaction
and the use of polite fiction. Rebellion is not at
all a new thing with him, nor was it with some of the
other isolates. They had established intolerance
for social compromise long before they came to Mayfair.

However, it is here that they face the most difficult adjustment. The life world is constricted
compared to what many had experienced in earlier
life, and the people with whom they must have the
most frequent contact over their fellow residents,
none of whom they have chosen. As we have noted,
the tolerance of the most tolerant and accepting
residents is challenged by the variety of people and
variety of conditions with which they must come to
terms daily. One can imagine the difficulties of the
intolerant person here. Constantly confronted with
people he or she wishes to avoid, and pressured to
participate in a staff dominated social program,
these people often see withdrawal as the only sol-
ution. Those isolates in the reality participation
circle 4 see the activities of Mayfair as tiny and
constricting. Those whose circle of reality is
narrower may simply not be able to get along with
staff and other residents. They will try to create
a separate life world for themselves within or aside
from the life world of Mayfair. Many, like Jack,
are all too aware that they are living in a life
world which is inimical to the way they wish to
live. Most of the isolates who are not senile are
angry. Most are aware that the price of non-participation is powerlessness in the life of the hotel
and loneliness, for they will find few people to
socialize with.

The non-participators in social life are not
aware of the price of non-participation, they are

aware of the price of participation--certainly they speak more of this than those who participate. Although this has been partially discussed in the chapters on leadership and relations with staff, it would be useful to reformulate it here in contrast with the price of non-participation. Participants in the social life of Mayfair and especially the resident leaders must be expert in maintaining the acceptable reality of the life world. They must be optimistic supporters of the philosophy of active retirement. They must deny for themselves and others anything which suggests that this is not true or possible at Mayfair. As we have discussed in the chapter on reality maintenance, they must systematically deal with a variety of threats every day. They must cooperate with staff.

Discussion of the past with the most important resident leaders showed that in every case, the individual had been a "community minded" person for most of his or her life. None had ever been the "loner" type. All discussed things and projects outside of family life with which they had been successfully involved in the past. These leaders usually would not talk about the compromises which their active involvement in social life and their leadership positions entailed. A few complained of the slowness or unwillingness of staff to consider resident-proposed change. A few found staff overbearing at times, but few would admit that social life was, to a great extent, dominated by staff.

Helping staff is the main cost of being involved actively in social life at Mayfair. Backing them up and helping with social events was what had to be done if one wanted the staff respect necessary to emerge as a resident leader. They must <u>never</u> be troublesome to staff. A woman with a strong personality, Helen Zimmer, had aspirations to become a leader at Mayfair. A few weeks after her arrival at Mayfair she began to speak up at meetings, criticize things, and to quarrel occasionally with those who disagreed with her. She sensed that contact with staff was one way to attain a position of influence with the residents. Therefore, she began to haunt the office of the Social Director. She came with suggestions, ideas, complaints, etc., and was always to be seen going through the office door. At first, the Social Director was delighted

147

as she wants people to be "lively," but as the weeks
passed she became weary of Helen's constant initia-
tion of contact with her. She began to send her
away saying that she couldn't listen now because
there was "work to be done." She put Helen off more
and more until it was obvious what was happening.
Helen became bitter and went around saying that she
'heard we would soon have a new Social Director." It
turned out that her wishful thinking proved correct.
A new Social Director came and Helen, learning from
past experience, set out to make a good impression.
She never went in to talk about complaints, but only
to "ask if she could help." She cut down the number
of times per week that she consulted the Social
Director, and when the research was ended she was
on her way to being thought a "helpful" person,
rather than a pest.

Being helpful to staff, maintaining the acceptable side of the life world, and attending and supporting social events are required of the resident
leaders. Not being a pest and attending planned
events are required of anyone who wants to be a part
of the social world at Mayfair. Both leaders and
resident participants in social life must not talk
about their lack of decision-making power too often.
All can complain from time to time, but constant
reiteration of this idea leads to exclusion from
social life. The philosophy of active retirement
does not have room for thoughts that one's life
is dominated by staff. Belonging to the social life
of the planned activities at Mayfair involves a
philosophy not unlike that of a rather strict political party. One can grumble a bit occasionally,
but one must support the party platform at all
costs. This is the price of participation; it is
the price which Jack and other isolates are unwilling to pay.

1. Simmons (1960) tries to define the main interests of the aging, using cross-cultural data. He names five interests which he considers to be universal--longer life, rest, prerogatives, participation, and an easy and honorable release. He feels that they can all be summed up under the terms "influence" and "security." Certainly the type of power sought by the Mayfair residents can be considered as "prerogatives" and "influence," and the lack of these made many residents very bitter.

2. The situation was different in the retirement communities described by Kleemeier (1954), Hoyt (1954), and Johnson (1971). Kleemeier reports that at Moosehaven, a retirement village run by the Order of Moose, all of the residents who were able had significant jobs to do, and that there was a great deal of self-determination. Hoyt states that in the trailer park he describes, all leadership in activities came from the residents, although the management sponsored the activities. Johnson, describing a trailer park in California, noted the strong leadership role of the Resident's Association there.

3. Burgess (1954) found correspondence between the level of social relations at Moosehaven, and the social status of the individual. He names three main types of social situations which characterize the elderly inhabitants: (1) isolates; (2) intimates; and (3) leaders. The isolates are cut off from much social life, the intimates have a few friends, and the leaders have many friends and acquaintances. The highest social positions within the retirement community are held by the leaders, with intimates and isolates in successively lower positions.

4. Williams and Loeb (1968) discuss the possibility that successful aging might be maintaining an optimal position in one's "social life space" in relation to his biological and psychological capacities, the "social life space" being a social map of interactions taking into account number, intensity, and complexity of interactions. The rather set nature of social relations at a retirement hotel might well be lacking in the intensity and complexity which would make life richer for

some of the residents.

     5. Acceptance of the philosophy and program of the hotel was necessary for participation in social life. Goffman (1961) saw the dilemma of the mental patient as similar, although more acute. "To get out of the hospital, or to ease their life within it, they must show acceptance of the place accorded to them, and the place accorded to them is to support the occupational role of those who appear to force this bargain" (1961:386).

CHAPTER X

THE TRIUMPH OF SOCIABILITY: MEANING AND

COMMUNITY WITHOUT POWER

There are no happy endings to this research, but rather a sense of amazement at the extreme strength of the human being in the search for interpersonal communication and meaning. There are great problems which prevent Mayfair House from being an ideal old-age community. Differences in reality participation circles sometimes close residents off from one another. The structure of reality of the life world is easily threatened and in need of constant defense. We have already shown that the residents lack power and often engage in pretense to hide this fact from themselves.

Also, these people are old and must devote a great deal of time to adjusting to this fact physically and psychologically. They are trying to create a new lifestyle for themselves late in life when changes are harder to make and when the tendency is to try to maintain a lifestyle consistent with that of earlier years. While they are trying to retain the integrity of their personalities, they must also face physical ills and life in a new society. When one considers all of these problems, the Mayfair residents' success in creating meaning and community is extraordinary.

A world of meaning and a communicating society exist at Mayfair House in spite of the lack of power of the residents. Creation of a life world does not depend upon the power of the participants to dominate the situation. A life world without adequate self-determination for its members is flawed, but it is not meaningless for those members. Its categories must take the power structure into account and must deal with it either overtly or covertly. Life could be richer in meaning for the residents if they had more opportunities for self-determination. Nevertheless, all but the most severely senile expressed the feeling that they were a part of a community and live a shared life with the other residents. They shared values, symbols, and most importantly, they shared common problems. Reality participation circle determined the degree of extension of an individual's world, but each circle had links with the other circles so there were always points of contact and sharing.

There were tensions and frustrations among the residents, but this never obliterated the sense that all were sharing a common life. Difficulties in communication made cooperation hard at times, but the residents continued to try to communicate with one another and to try to help one another. I found that often the verbal expression of resentment was as far as a resident went. He or she would complain about their fellow residents, but continue to communicate with them and to spend a great deal of time with them.

For every person who rudely pushed his way into a crowded elevator, two could be found who would say: "You go first, I'll wait. I've got no place to hurry to." People who were missing from dining room tables were checked on by their table mates. One day I walked with a woman to a nearby hospital to visit a friend. The woman was so dizzy herself that she had to be held firmly and had to stop to rest about every half block. When I suggested that she could go another time, she said: "Oh no, I promised Lizzie I'd be there today! I can't disappoint her!" One volunteer got up at six in the morning so that she could telephone other residents who had early appointments at the local clinic. For all the talk and resentment about not wanting a "nursing home atmosphere" there were many residents who wore themselves out caring for others. Some of those who complained the loudest about "not wanting that sort of person here" were the quickest to help a helpless fellow resident. All the people at times turned away from sickness and death, but many turned back to help.

There was grumbling, but aid and kindness seemed almost instinctive to many of the residents. One was almost inclined to agree with Kropotkin (1902) who saw mutual aid among animals and men as a primary factor in evolution. He saw this as operating in opposition to the struggle for existence by individual creatures and species. Sociability was seen to be an instinct which men and animals share leading them to help one another. He says:

> It is a feeling infinitely wider than love or sympathy--an instinct that has been slowly developed among animals and men in the course of an extremely long evolution and which has taught animals and man alike the force they can borrow from the practice of mutual aid and the joys they can find in social life (Kropotkin 1902:xiii).

Whether we wish to view mutual aid as an instinct or as a survival strategy which men have learned through ages of living together, it manifested itself strongly at Mayfair House. It manifested itself in a situation which often made it difficult for people to sustain a desire to do something for others. It is a place in which a great many frustrations and situations which no one can change arise. Difficulties in communication among people with different reality participation circles causes constant irritation. Nevertheless, the process of living has caused a common life world to emerge at Mayfair.

Although the life world at Mayfair is in a constant process of change, at any single point in time it represents a "given" to which new and old residents must adapt themselves. What are the most outstanding qualities of the life world and what are the residents' response to them?

First of all, Mayfair House is a total environment with a philosophy of retirement put forward by management, staff, and resident leaders. Each new resident must deal with the environment and also decide what sort of response to make to the philosophy of retirement. As we have already discussed, Mayfair House is committed to the idea of an active retirement. The management believe that the more activities an older person engages in, the happier he or she will be. Participation is very strongly urged. So much so that the old person who has led a quiet and sheltered life may find himself considered to be something of a deviant in this setting although he was not so considered so before. The active club-joining person has a better chance to continue his former mode of life and still get social approval from the new group. There are few alternatives to the active life for a "good" retirement in Mayfair House terms.

Another aspect of the Mayfair life world is the extremely varied group of residents. Unlike facilities for a certain religion or nationality, there are all religions, races, and ethnic backgrounds represented here. Also, there are a variety of reality participation circles represented among the residents. Similarity of both background and reality participation circle is extrememly hard to find. Residents must look hard to find people with whom they have something in common, other than age.

Still another aspect of the life world is the absence of real power for the residents. This is the situation which makes for problems in recruiting resident "leaders." Those who are alert and interested enough to fill these roles are usually also acute enough to see that their "leadership" positions are something of a travesty. This leads to the necessity for insincerity and playacting, which some very able residents are reluctant to become involved in. Also, attempt to bring about change are more likely to bring about frustration than the desired results. There is too much domination of all aspects of life by staff. There are too few areas where residents can make their own decisions and carry them through.

Because the conception of the "good" retirement at Mayfair is rather limited, and because there is no real power for the residents, there are a limited number of roles open to them. They must try to find an available one which is compatible with the personality which they have spent a lifetime building up. There are four main catogories of roles which wc oan use to describe the response of all of the residents to the situation. Within each category there are possibilities of differentiation, but all possibilities will remain in the general category. The categories of roles are as follows:

    (1) Active, helpful (to staff)
    (2) Non-active, cooperative
    (3) Active, rebellious
    (4) Non-active, non-cooperative
On the basis of former life and response to the new situation, each resident will assume one of these roles at the hotel. Oncc assumed, it is

hard to change as the person will be already cate-
gorized. The following descriptions show how these
roles were represented by four Mayfair residents.

Hilda Reilly--The Ideal Retired Person

Role 1--Active, helpful

We have already described Hilda and the fact
that she is considered by staff and most residents
to be exactly what a retired person should be. She
is very active in the hotel activities and in volunteer work outside the hotel. She is about 75
years old but in good health. She is very well
dressed and always cheerful. Her main characteristic is her constant optimism . She was never heard
to say anything bad about another resident, and yet
she did not have an air of "trying to be charitable.
She seems to be genuinely interested in everyone
and to really see the best points about everyone.

Hilda Reilly had worked all of her life and
she never married. She was bookkeeper to a small
firm and a "helper" to her sister who had many
children. A native-born American, she had lived
most of her life in the Middle West and did not
want to leave it. She had always been active in
her church and had always maintained her own home
in a small but very nice apartment. Committee work
at Mayfair was natural to her as she had always
been active in her community. Activity, work, and
involvement are the three most important things to
Hilda and these, along with her personal qualities
make her life at Mayfair a good one. Buhler (1961)
would have seen Hilda as a person whose retirement
was meaningful because her life had been meaningful.

Both staff and residents know they can depend
on her--residents for help in anything, and staff
for her constant participation in social and cultura
events. She almost never missed a meeting and she
always attended the planned programs. She is like
an active grandmother to everyone and is very well
loved. She is not a person who appears to need
to have power over others, therefore her life at
Mayfair brings contentment. She is free to pursue
her main interest which is people, and the appreciation which she is given is confirmation that
her life style has meaning. She is aware that she
is to a certain extent, a symbol for the other

residents and is careful to live up to this responsibility. She never expresses negative feelings
about anything, and people come to her to be cheered
up. In many ways her later years may be the most
meaningful of her life, for she is needed, appreciated,
and loved.

Mary Krasula--One of the Nice People

Role 2--Non-active, cooperative

Mary is a quiet person, fond of people, but
fond of being alone as well. She likes her immaculate room at Mayfair and works to keep it that way.
She is sociable and always seems to be smiling. She
does not take an active role in the committees
and activities, but she does attend most meetings
and entertainments and always enjoys them. She has
a few friends that she talks with each day, and she
writes many letters to her large family. She is
85 years old and she feels that it is good to be
retired, good to be able to rest.

Mary is of Polish background, but she was
born in the United States and has forgotten most
of the Polish she learned as a child. She married
young (a man like herself, of Polish background) and
had five children, one of whom is now dead. Her
husband was a man who went from job to job and the
family had little real security. He died before
all of the children had finished school, making it
necessary for Mary to find work. She found a part-
time job in a company which made religious garments
for priests. The job became a full-time job and she
worked there until she retired. She was given a
big party and a proper send-off because she was one
of the most well-liked employees. Although she
thinks of herself mainly as a mother and grandmother,
she knows a great deal of the world of work outside
the home. This increases her enjoyment of her retirement as a time of well-earned rest.

She has few complaints about the hotel, and
she just avoids people who seem incompatible. People
who know her are very fond of her, and those who do
not will always say that she "looks nice." Mary is
well liked by staff who know that she can be counted
on to be at most entertainments and who know that
she will never be any trouble to them. She is not
active but she is happy and has a cooperative atti-

tude which is very good for creating a pleasant atmosphere. Not interested in seeking a leadership position, Mary helps make a pleasant background at Mayfair. She is rewarded by the approval of staff and her friends, and is able to live life the way she likes to.

Jack Stein--Waiting for the Revolution to Start

Role 3--Active, rebellious

We have already met Jack Stein, the 82-year-old rebel who hates institutions and despises people who live in them. He lives at Mayfair House because he has to live somewhere and the hotel suits his budget.

Jack Stein was born in a small town in Russia and he remembers it very well, although he was a young child when he came to the United States. He also remembers the Russian language--unlike many of the other residents who came here from Europe as children. He would often make remarks about people who claimed to be from Russia when they could not speak Russian. His English is also excellent and he is very good at describing things in a colorful way.

Jack had done many things in his life--mainly as a small businessman. He never married but he was very fond of the children and grandchildren of his old partner who is now dead. He did not think of himself as a "family" sort of person and would often talk about the "wild" things he had done when he was younger. When he was depressed he would complain that he had "never done anything right" but when he was feeling better he would enjoy talking about the variety of things that he had done. Other members of his family had been more successful in the standard interpretation of the word. One brother was a doctor while another was a very successful business man. He was conscious of being something of a black sheep--a role he sometimes hated and sometimes enjoyed.

In conversation one gets the feeling that he would rather be almost anywhere than here. He looks down upon the staff and most of the people who feels are his intellectual inferiors. He is very intelligent, and this is a handicap in the situation because he can see through all the pretense and

playacting and he refuses to take part in it. This
isolates him from much of the social life, and
alienates many residents as well. Staff regard
him with suspicion, for he is too sharp to be
labelled "senile" and too difficult to be "handled."
He sees himself as an iconoclast, and frequently
goes about telling people how "lousy" everything
at the hotel really is. This makes him unpopular
with staff and with many residents. He always over-
states the case, but the kernels of truth in his
pronouncements are real enough to make people uncomfortable. He does not consider the staff to be authorities, but to be "nobodies" who have no right to
tell him what to do. He would love to lead a
residents revolt, but he has no following. He has
the qualities of a leader, but he is too abrasive
to be successful. He would quarrel too much with
his followers. He is also too extreme to attract
the Mayfair residents, most of whom just want a
peaceful life. He is lonely, angry, and very much
alive. He has no outlet for his particular talents,
and his personality type is not appreciated at Mayfair House.

Bob Brown--Did I Have Dinner or Not?

Role 4, Non-Active
non-cooperative

Bob Brown is 76 years old, mild mannered, and
completely lost. Ever since he came to live at Mayfair six months ago he has been confused. He eats
at the first meal setting, but often forgets that
he has eaten and reappers at the second.

Bob Brown was for many years the owner of a
hardware store. It was a small but adequate business. He and his wife had two sons who eventually
moved to another part of the country. All went
well until Bob lost his wife six years ago. After
that he was very lonely and decided to sell the
business and retire. He went on a couple of long
holidays, and fulfilled his lifelong dream to go to
Europe and to the Middle East. He still shows his
Passport with great pride. However, Bob began having health problems--one after another. Finally,
a stroke put him in the hospital for a long stay.
When he came out, his sons decided that he would
be better off in a hotel like Mayfair where he
would not have to worry about cooking or shopping
for groceries. When he moved in to Mayfair his

physical recovery from the stroke was complete, but
he had terrible memory problems. He cannot remember
what he has done in the course of a day.

When he first came, he said, nearly weeping: "I'm
confused today, can't figure out where I am. Things
were all right at my old apartment, but here I feel
funny. Just give me a few days to get straight."
He has never gotten straight, but spends his days
asking other people questions, trying to figure
things out. He will wander about the hotel asking
what day it is, what time it is, or even occasionally, "How did I get here?" His disorientation does
not seem to improve. He is treated kindly by most
people and barely tolerated by others. The most
upsetting thing is the perpetually confused expression on his face. He is really suffering and trying
to figure things out. He is not non-cooperative
on purpose. He is simply unable to be cooperative
because he's not sure what is happening.

Occasionally, a kind person or staff member will
sit down with him and try to clarify everything. For
about five minutes all seems better, and then he
forgets again. He cannot really be part of the social
life. He will wander into meetings and then wander
out because they confuse him. Entertainments do
little to cheer him because he is too busy trying
to figure out what has happened. Contacts with
other residents have little meaning for him because they do not really reach him. Staff find him
rather trying, although they attempt to be patient.
His life seems to be a fruitless search for clarifi-
cation of his situation. He is physically present,
but not present mentally or emotionally. His confusion is disturbing to others as well, and most
people try to avoid talking to him. He is a negative
element in the atmosphere of the hotel.

In describing these four residents we have gone
from what is considered best in a resident to what
is considered worst. "Best" and "worst" are from the
point of view of the large part of the residents and
from the point of view of the staff. Hilda Reilly,
active and helpful is almost ideal, and Mary Krasula,
non-active but cooperative and pleasant is definitely
desirable as a resident. Jack Stein was considered
to be a negative personality, but at least he was
active and spent most of the day away from the hotel.
Bob Brown is pitiful. He could not really go any-

where else, so he spent all the days at the hotel, hopelessly trying to get people to tell him something which would make things clearer to him. He is one of the people that the other residents say gives the place a "nutty" atmosphere. Jack Stein is an active rebel, and Bob Brown is non-active and non-cooperative. Bob has no place in the social life. Neither has Jack, but he has at least played an active role in rejecting it himself.

The established norms of the life world of Mayfair rank these different types of responses to life there on a continuum of "worst" to "best." The norms have evolved through the continual interaction of staff and residents and their reactions to the philosophy of retirement to which the hotel is committed. Klein (1956) whose work is firmly based upon that of Homans(1951) says this about the evolution of norms.

> By an individual's set of norms we mean all the
> standards, whether practical or moral which
> lead him to rank one man or one action as
> preferable to another in a given set of cir-
> cumstances (Klein 1956:76).

In the case of Mayfair Hotel, the practical and the moral become mixed in the evaluation of the different types of acting in the situation. The active, helpful person is validated by the extra notice he receives from residents and the small share of power he gets from the staff. His actions are practical in that they make his life better and they are also "good" because they conform to the high values placed upon active participation. The "out of it" and helpless people like Bob Brown are pitied but also looked down upon because they "shouldn't be that way." Senility is greatly feared by the clear-minded residents and there is some confusion as to whether it is something that just happens or if it is something that happens when people "let themselves go." Most of the active people felt that senility was caused by vegetating and that it was something which would creep up on one if one didn't "keep active." Thus, there is some feeling that senility is something that a person allows to happen, and therefore he can be blamed for it to a certain extent. There is real confusion here, for some people will say of a Bob Brown, "Poor man, it could happen to anyone!" and mean it.

From another point of view, each response to the life at Mayfair can be considered to be a particular personality's method of dealing with the situation there. Murphy (1976) gives the clearest definition to the individual's attempts to face life under the term "coping." This concept, as she uses it, is twofold. It concerns the individual's means of meeting the challenges, frustrations, difficulties, etc., of his environment, and secondly, it concerns the individual's ability to remain integrated with his total environment. Although both aspects of coping are adaptive, the first emphasizes actions taken by the individual and the second emphasizes the mechanisms within the individual which allow him to remain in harmony with the world outside. Coping is not merely a passive adjusting to circumstances, but it is an individual's strategy for mastering his relations with the world. It is his choice of the means of relating to events and people which concern him.

In a very important sense, the four role types which we have described as encompassing all of the types of response at Mayfair, are four different methods of coping with the life world there. An individual's choice of which type of role his behavior will approach is not fortuitous. It is based upon his or her entire past. It is based upon former social position, sex, family, community, as well as upon the old person's evaluation of the scene at Mayfair. As so many have pointed out, in old age the patterns of life are not changed. They remain consistent with those of former life, although there are some changes which age alone can bring. Coping patterns are the same. Each individual tried to adapt strategies which he or she had used before to fit the situation at Mayfair. The set of norms operative at Mayfair valued some strategies higher than others and so certain individuals were better prepared by their past lives for a retirement of the Mayfair sort.

Long discussion with people representing the four role types showed that they were using long established patterns of behavior--trying to make them work for the present situation. Hilda Reilly had always been involved with club and volunteer work and from talking with her it became clear that even when she had been busy with a career of office work, these activities had been the main focus of her

interest. The situation at Mayfair, with its need for
active retirees was ideal for her. She was rewarded
with praise for doing what she had always done and
what she felt best doing.

Mary Krasula had always led a quiet life and she
kept up that pattern at Mayfair. She found that her
natural good nature was a definite asset at Mayfair
where cheerfulness was a most treasured value. She
had worked outside the home, only when it had been
financially necessary. Her real life had always
been centered upon family activities. It remained
so at Mayfair. Letters and photographs from children and grandchildren were the most important things
in her world. She did not see herself as needing to
be active in the social program, although she
attended events and enjoyed them. Staff and residents
valued her quiet good cheer and cooperativeness.
Her carry-over of her former life pattern was successful.

Jack Stein, too, successfully maintained the
activity patterns of former life. He was always
a "loner" and proud of the fact. Social life was
always a set of compromises to him. As he has grown
older he probably treasures his few good friends
more, but this does not prevent him from "telling
them off" if he wishes. Discussing his former life
with him, one is struck by the number of times he
found it necessary to break with someone because
he did not like what they did. He was never good at
compromise. Thus, he evolved a role as a rebel for
himself. He is rebel who is always searching for
human contact, but who has always hated established
forms of social life. He sees himself as a social
critic, and sustains this role rather well because
although exaggerated, his comments usually have some
truth to them. He is not a part of the social life
of the hotel, but he does have some people with
whom he talks and he has established himself as a
local character in the social world of Mayfair.
When he was ill at the local hospital he said: "I
got a card signed by quite a few of the Mayfair residents. Gee, I thought they all hated me!" He was
surprised to find that people knew that he was ill
and troubled to send a card. Actually, he was
well established in a role as the hotel's main eccentric. He was tolerated because he is clear-minded
and there are not too many like him.

Bob Brown was too much unaware of what was going

on around him to be considered to be using his confused role as a coping device. However, there were
many others, much more aware of the situation who
found that helplessness was their most effective response to the situation. It was not truly effective,
because it did not always bring the desired results,
but for many residents it was the only way they knew
to try to control the situation in which they found
themselves. One woman went around asking people to
help her with various things which went wrong in her
room. She was extremely irritating, but she usually
got attention, and even staff would try to help her
so that she would leave them alone. Others would
ask questions--"What time it it?" "What day is it?"
etc.--forcing others to respond to them. The helpless role was despised by most of the residents and
was only adopted by those who had not other possible
way of acting. As a coping device it was the least
desirable and least effective one of all.

The sympathy and sociability which I observed
at Mayfair in spite of all difficulties existed perhaps largely because of the unspoken realization of
the residents that they were all trying in their own
ways to cope with the problems of being old, living
closely with others, and their lack of power in
society and at the hotel. As we have see, some
methods of coping were approved and gave maximum
results, while others were less successful. Nevertheless, all of the residents saw that they were
struggling with the same problems. Different reality participation circles did divide people, but
they were considered to be what they in fact were,
different methods of facing life. Like the different role types, they made it hard for some people
to communicate effectively, but did not remove the
conviction that all of the residents were "in the
same fight." Active residents looked down upon
helpless ones and said, "They shouldn't be here!"
but they felt responsible for them. Their own
identification with one another gave a bitter edge
to the remarks made upon the senile and helpless
residents. Also, a desire that others should be
kind if one "got that way" made the active residents
conscientious in looking after the others. A sense
of belonging to a group was there even in those who
swore that they did not want to belong to such a
group. Many times, residents seemed to feel that
they were a group in opposition to the staff. Staff
monopoly of power was irritating to all, and gave

them a common bond of resentment.

In Chapter IV we discussed the problem of vast differences in the reality participation circles of the residents, showing how this situation can lead to conversations without much communication. This is very true, but it is well to consider the other side of the picture, too. There may well be a great deal of meaning communicated in a meaningless conversation. The main thing which is communicated, even in the most ridiculous exchange, is the _desire_ to communicate. Residents know that they need one another in very basic ways, and attempt to establish bridges of communication continue, despite discouraging results which might make many a younger person give up. Valiant attempts to bridge differences in reality participation circles, ethnic group, religion, interests, and even language took place constantly. The efforts of some residents to understand and to be understood was astounding. As we have shown, even the convinced rebels like Jack Stein were constantly talking and searching for more conversations.

Like the mutual aid and support which the residents offer one another, the constant attempt for communication went on even when people said that they had "no one to talk with." As everyone who has ever spent time in a country where one does not speak the language knows, belief that it is possible to communicate, and repeated attempts to show one's meaning, are necessary for survival. The efforts of the Mayfair residents show each other their good will and their desire to communicate meaning, went on in spite of the most discouraging results. To an important extent, shared meaning was shared desire for communication as well as certain shared ideas about the world. Commitment to communication was one of the most important values held in common by the residents at Mayfair. The following dialogue will show the intensity of some of the attempts at communication:

Mrs. Able(No. 4 reality participation circle):
      Hello there Mrs. Green. How are you
      today? It looks like better weather.

Mrs. Green(No. 1 reality participation circle and not
      feeling at all well):
      What's that you said? How I am? Well,
      who knows--all I do is ache.

Mrs. Smith (No. 1 R.P.C.): You ache! I though I'd never get out of bed, but have you tried Ben Gay? Sometimes it helps a little.

Mrs. Able: Don't you think the better weather will make you both feel better? When it's dry there is not so much pain from arthritis. Also, I've been reading that there's a new cure. I think you take hormones.

Mrs. Green: I hear that hormones can be bad too. I don't know what is worse, the disease or the medicine.

Mrs. Smith: Why don't you try my "Ben Gay."

Bob Brown (R.P.C. No. 1 and confused): Does anyone know whether I had lunch or not?

Mrs. Green: What! How would I know if you had lunch?

Mrs. Able: I think you had lunch Bob, because I saw you come out of the dining room about forty minutes ago.

Mrs. Green: He drives you nuts with his questions, but I guess we should try to help him. (To Bob Brown) How is your daughter, Bob?

Bob Brown: I don't know, I haven't seen her in months.

Mrs. Smith: What are you talking about. She was here yesterday and you had lunch with her in the dining room. I say you. I noticed because she had on such a pretty red suit. Do you mean to say you don't remember!

Bob: Yeah, it kind of slipped my mind, but I'm really glad to know she came. Did she have a good time?

Mrs. Able: She certainly looked as if she were having a good time. She was very glad to see you. I noticed that she talked with the social director for a long time She wants you to be happy here.

Bob: Gosh, it just slipped my mind. Thanks a lot for telling me.

Mr. Peck (No. 3 R.P.C. and a hotel politician): Nutty as a fruitcake, old Bob, but he used to be a business man. Had his own store. Are you coming to the House Maintenance meeting tonight, Edna (to Mrs. Able)?

Mrs. Able: Sure, I wouldn't miss this one. They're going to discuss the new roses for the patio.

Mrs. Green: I don't like the patio. Everytime I go out there someone is sitting where I want to sit.

Mrs. Able: Then you should sit somewhere else until the person leaves and then take the chair you want.

Mr. Peck: What we need is some sort of occupancy time for the patio chairs. Some people never get a chair. What's the use of being old if we can't sit in the sun, right Bob?

Bob: What's that? What did you say?

Mr. Peck: I said, we old people ought to be able to sit in the sun.

Bob: Oh yes, there's a place here where you sit outside. I like it.

Mrs. Green: Sun is good for my bones.

Mr. Peck: Then be sure to come to the meeting tonight. We're going to ask for more chairs and see if those stingy devils will send us some.

Mrs. Green: I'll come. I hate to be inside when the weather's nice. I want more chairs too--near the roses.

Mrs. Smith: It's no use going to meetings. Nothing ever gets done.

Mr. Peck: We all know that Annie, but we have
              to keep on trying, don't we?

Mrs. Able: Thank the Lord for people like Mr. Peck
              who look out for everybody's interest.
              Who knows what would happen here without
              them. They keep an eye on the staff.
              At least we still get dessert with our
              meals. Mrs. Food Services was saying
              she thought we'd have to give up some
              desserts to save money.

Bob: I like dessert, but I miss a lot of
              meals because I forget to go in for them.
              But when I go, I want the dessert.

Mr. Peck: Right Bob! You won't lose your dessert
              while I can still fight.

Mrs. Green: It's time for our lunch sitting. I can
              hear them going in. Don't forget to go
              to the early dinner sitting, Bob!

Bob(looking at Mr. Peck): I wish I could sit with
              him. I'd feel a lot better about gettin
              my dessert.

Mrs. Able: Don't worry, we all get dessert, or no
              one does. We all get the same meals.

Mr. Peck: That's right! Ha Ha! We're all in the
              same leaky boat!

Mrs. Able: As long as we can keep it afloat.....
              well, let's go............

     The conversations go on day after day, building
a world in which communication exists against tremendous odds. The barriers between people exist
and the talking goes on, building understanding and
somehow making all of the problems easier to bear.
Facing death as we all do, the people at Mayfair talk
to pass the time and to keep away the dark.

     As the study of Mayfair was completed, it seems
obvious that many more in depth studies of old
people in retirement communities and in the larger
community are needed. The statistical aspects of
old age are well documented, and many "how to" works
on setting up retirement homes and facilities with
health care are available. What is lacking .

167

is long-term studies of old people acting in society, solving their economic and health problems, and expressing their reactions to the process of aging. The aging person as an individual has been fairly well documented, although more comparisons of old age patterns in relation to patterns established earlier in life are needed. What has not been thoroughly studied is the ways in which old people live together in society. Many students of the aged have seen a lessening of degree and intensity of all social' contacts (see Barker 1968, Buhler 1961, Cumming 1961, Henry 1961). What is the character of the social life which remains to the aging person? What are the differences in quality, if any, between the social life of an elderly person and a younger person? This must be studied through months of close contact with a group of elderly people, for while quantity of social life may be documented through questionnaires, it is far harder to discover _quality_ of social life this way. The Mayfair material suggests that while social life there, as elsewhere, is concerned with building reality and validating social claims of individuals, it may be more concerned with communication for the sake of communication than among younger groups. Cumming and Henry (1961) and Cumming (1975) suggest that there is a change in the "style" of an elderly person's interaction. Rewards sought are different and role orientation lessens. This seems to be confirmed by the research at Mayfair House. The patience shown by the resident in trying to establish contact with others with different reality participation circles and different interests, backgrounds, and conditions of health, shows that here talking and trying to communicate seemed to be a more important value than in the society at large. When the research was begun, a staff member said: "They'll be glad to talk to you. They'll talk you to death. You won't be able to get away."

It was true that almost every resident wanted very much to talk, but to talk in the sense of meaningful communication. Knowledge of the social structure, reality structure came out of conversations. Among old people one becomes more aware than ever of the importance of words. Human life is built with words and the old are very knowledgeable about this fact. That is why so many conversations at Mayfair were focused upon "What did he say?" more than upon "what did he do?" We need more studies which concentrate upon the conversations of old people in connection with their social life. Words define the values which support the social forms and particularly in the exclusively old age community a somewhat specialized vocabulary may be used to define social reality. For example, the words "active" and "out of it" at Mayfair were the polar opposites describing what a retired person should and should not be. More study of any special vocabulary among older people would shed light on their particular type of social life and reality.

In studies of old age facilities, particular attention should be paid to the relations between residents and staff. Enough work has been done to indicate that Kleemeier (1961), Byrne (1974) describe situations in which the retired person felt that he or she had a great deal of freedom to decide things which were important. At Mayfair there was no real power and little significant decision-making for the residents. As a result, a number of problems arose which made for frustration and difficulty in finding a satisfactory life. Some of the unfortunate types of relations between staff and residents similar to those described by Goffman (1961) for his "total institution" were observed.

Relations between old people themselves should be recorded in detail from observations made over time. Kingsley Amis' (1974) novel Ending Up, a satirical story of five old people living together in Tuppenny-hapenny Cottage, is exaggerated in its events,but the conversations ring true. The mutual need of all of the characters for one another, and the scheme of living they have evolved are real. Their sense of being both forgotten and "put down" by the younger people is also real. The conversations bring understanding of the old peoples' problems and also make one understand their behavior and their relations with younger people. The bitterness and spitefulness which illness and other frustrations can bring are well described. The following quotation describes one of the members' analysis of his feelings and actions toward the others:

He would not have said that he found the company at Tuppenny-happenny Cottage altogether without savor. There was still a little satisfaction to be had out of scoring off them in talk, but

it did seem to be on the decrease. He must
see if he could not come up with some less
subtle means of venting on the four of them
his lack of respect and affection. What had
happened, what was the change in his circumstances which had led him to this decision? Well,
anyhow, such a project would help to pass the
time (Amis 1974:75).

Although this is a novel rather than a sociological
or anthropological work, the descriptions are the
kind which we need in these fields for a more complete picture of old age and the ways in which old
people live. The general background material of
the subject has become fuller and fuller. We
need the close focus of detailed information on
specific situations, on what specific old people
do and say and how they arrange their lives.

CONCLUSIONS

This work deals with the means by which a meaningful life world is created in a community of the elderly which draws its members from many different backgrounds within the larger society. Status in the community and a certain amount of self-determination are determined by the individual's participation in hotel social groups and by his "endorsement" by staff. Residents have large areas of shared meaning despite constant problems of communication with one another as a result of participation in different reality circles. The values of the residents stress work, being "active," and "acting young," which indicates to me that the concentration of old people together in this case has not led to the formation of values very different from those held by large numbers of younger people in the wider society. No specific "old folks values" seemed to be emerging in this community although mutual sympathy was important. The case of the woman who shouted: "I hate old people" was not an isolated one. One constantly heard "He's an old fool," "People don't grow wiser as they grow older, they grow more stupid," and similar comments. Being old was a negative value to almost all of the residents, although there were exceptions. The importance of work as a source of prestige cannot be stressed too strongly. Control over "public opinion," privileges from staff, and a sense of worthiness came from work on committees, work with staff, or other work such as doing tailoring jobs for other residents (see Kleemeier 1951).

The residents' lives are largely controlled by the staff. They were often resentful of this fact, but perceived it as being no different from the type of relationship that they had already experienced with younger people in the world outside Mayfair House. Many residents complained that their sons, daughters, or other younger relatives "thought they knew everything" and tried to tell them what to do. Jack Stein's fury at being told to put on a tie by a young staff member was a case which showed the real feeling among the old here that younger people try to push them around. The fact that the staff seemed always to be very busy was not surprising to the residents who had found their children and relatives often "too busy" for much visiting. Many residents found much more opportunity for socializing and conversation than they had had while living in their children's homes. Although there was no formation of specifically "old folks values," there was a kind of solidarity and a sense of "we old people" in opposition to "those younger ones." This distinction was an important part of the life world at Mayfair.

Communication through conversation is the main means by which the life world is built. Social structure, interest groups, and staff-resident relations are the conditions which limit, but do not dictate, the evolution of the shared world of meaning. None of the background conditions remain constant. The domination of most situations by staff was effectively countered by residents in numerous ploys on other occasions. Coping with the situation involved different techniques for different occasions. Some were more successful than others, but there was always a dynamic tension in any interaction situation and the outcome could be one of a number of possible ones. An important part of the shared life world was mutual awareness of the coping devices which people in each reality participation circle were using both to improve their feelings of self-determination and their ability to act independently.

This study is a traditional anthropological community study. It is unusual as an ethnography because it concerns itself with a community in which young people are conspicuously absent, except for the staff. I felt that the problem of building a life world was best studied in a community in which the only factor common to all residents was the fact that all are old having come from very diverse backgrounds. When individuals are removed (either forcibly or by choice) from the communities in which they have spent their lives they come to the new community somewhat as refugees with only their memories and their past techniques of coping with life. They enter what is in many ways a new culture. Culture building in the sense of creation of social structure, values, symbols, and roles is constantly taking place in the retirement hotel, for the population is replaced at a greater speed than in the wider society because of the age of the residents. There was a chance to observe culture shock as new residents came in, and change as old ones died or became too ill to retain their leadership roles, and new people emerged into influential positions. The high death rate seemed to speed everything, and it was as if, while sharing many characteristics of the wider society, the world of Mayfair operated socially at an accelerated rate of change.

Patterns of meaning and the shape of the life world were sought in the research. Repeated techniques for coping with powerlessness and feeling of powerlessness, and paterns of communication between the residents were sought. I felt that perhaps some regularities would emerge which we could see repeated in other old age communities. These could give insight into distinctive features of elderly life style in this culture, and in other cultures. The findings of the research are qualitative and descriptive. Elderly people brought together from diverse situations into an old age community create a life world which they share, and the values of which reflect those of the larger culture with certain differences. Status is not based upon money or control over material assets. It is based upon vigor, strong personality, and willingness to enter into a cooperative relationship with staff. Influence is based upon being seen as active, involved, and able to use staff and their power to further one's own ends. Communication for its own sake was perhaps more important at Mayfair than in the society outside. There was more talking just for the sake of being together.

The method of detailed analysis of the contents of conversations in building up the picture of social structure and the life world provides for intersubjectivity in the research. This method, I believe, yields results which could be justly compared with similar information from other old age communities, and in a variety of other community settings. The data sought is qualitative in nature, but the method has a specificity which would allow it to be duplicated in any setting. For example, a person's reality participation circle was determined by having at least three separate conversations with him and by counting the number of times he mentioned himself, close friends, hotel social life, or the outside world. Social status was determined for individuals by observing their reality participation circles, attendance and demeanor at social events, asking at least 25 other residents to "place" that individual in the social scheme, and finally, by asking the individual to "place" himself in the social scheme.

Much quantitative data which I would have liked to have had was denied to me as the hotel would not allow me to see their files. Information on amount of education, why a person had moved into the hotel, particulars of health, and exact financial situation were "confidential." Residents were asked to answer these same questions for my questionnaire, but I had reason to feel that I was not getting accurate data because many of them said quite different things on other occasions. They were assured that the questionnaires were confidential and that no names would be used, but the fact that they knew me made some of them try to improve their answers to give a better impression. For example, one man who told me that he had finished high school when he was asked for the questionnaire, later said: "Boy, I wish I had education like Mr. X (the Administrator)! I never even finished sixth grade!"

A better technique was to use the data given me by staff as regards income, etc., as a background to my own observations and conversations with the residents. Usually residents were eager to give information about themselves and even more eager to talk about other people. Comparing what a person said about himself with what a number of others said about him, gave a fairly accurate picture of his place in the total life world. Conversations gave a wealth of material about the speaker, the people he spoke about, life at the hotel, and his perceptions of life at the hotel. Intensive study of conversation in all its aspects is, I believe, one of the richest sources of ethnographic data and is a field in itself within Anthropology. Differences in old peoples' and younger peoples' conversations would add greatly to our appreciation of what is different in the life style of the elderly.

Although all intellectual constructs involve both deductive and inductive processes in their creation, the study of conversation both as a creator and describer of the life world is heavily inductive. The picture of the life world at Mayfair was built slowly piece by piece using conversation as the main, though not only, source of information. When the picture emerged it was a true picture, not because I as an observer stated it to be true, but because it

was a joint effort of seeing with the residents. My
observations were united with what they saw, through
our constant communication. There was no objective-
subjective distinction in the view of the life world.
It was an intersubjective reality which I came to
share and, although it was not my life world, it
became an important part of it.

In the field of Anthropology, the ethnography
of the elderly as a field of study has hardly begun.
I believe that this is a rich area to explore, for
relations between age categories and generations in
primitive cultures has an extensive literature. In
this culture the elderly are a group as distinct as
any ethnic or minority group, although they should
not be considered as one. They are an age category
discriminated against by many of the values of the
culture at large. They possess despised characteristics, such as dimished vitality, non-working status, negligible consumer group status, and especially
"oldness." They have consistently been considered
as a social problem, not studied as a group whose
position and role in society reflect society's
values.

We need to study the elderly in terms of their
total life style. More detailed ethnographies would
give material for comparing patterns of community
formation, communication, value retention, and addition of new values, late in life. Close focus and
analysis of both conversation and activities of the
elderly in old age communities and in the larger
community are necessary. We have enough generaliza-
tions and statistics about old people. We need
ethnographic information about all aspects of their
lives. If such information were available, the life
of the old in this culture could be compared mean-
ingfully with the life of the old in other cultures.
Styles of life for the old such as retirement hotels
could be compared with life in a family setting or
life alone, if adequate data were available. Comparisons of old age communities with institutions
such as boarding schools, jails, mental facilities,
hospitals, and nursing homes could yield interesting
information about coping patterns and means of finding some self-determination. These types of comparisons could give some idea of which life world patterns are characteristic of old people and which
are characteristic of all people who are fighting
a sense of powerlessness.

All of these areas lack significant ethnographic data. Long term observation, conversation and event analysis, and the placing of events and conversations against a background of social structure are the anthropological means which I feel would be most effective in extending our information on these communities which are still a new territory for anthropologists.

BIBLIOGRAPHY

Amis, Kingsley

1974   Ending Up. New York: Harcourt Brace
                Jovanovich.

Anderson, John E.

1960   Research on Aging. In Aging in Western
                Societies. E. Burgess, Ed. Chicago:
                University of Chicago Press.

Arensberg, Conrad

1965   Culture and Community. New York,
                Chicago, Burlingname: Harcourt Brace
                and World Inc.

Barker, Roger G. and Louise Shedd Barker

1968   The Psychological Ecology of Old People
                in Midwest, Kansas and Yoerdale, York-
                shire. In Middle Age and Aging: A
                Reader in Social Psychology. Bernice
                L. Neugarten, Ed. Chicago and London:
                Pp. 44-452.

Berger, Peter L.

1963   Invitation to Sociology: A Humanistic
                Perspective. Garden City, N.Y. Anchor
                Books: Doubleday and Co. Inc.

1967   The Sacred Canopy: Elements of a
                Sociological Theory of Religion. Garden
                City, N.Y.: Anchor Books. Doubleday
                and Co. Inc.

Blau, Zena S.

1961   Structural Constraint on Friendship in
                Old Age. American Sociological Review
                26 (3) : 429-431.

Buhler, Charlotte

1935   The Curve of Life as Studied in Bio-
               graphies. Journal of Applied Psychology
               19: 405-409.

1951   Maturation and Motivation. Personality
               1 : 184-211.

1959   Zur Psychologie des Menschlichen
               Lenesbenslauf. Psychologische Rundshau
               8: 1-15.

1961   Old Age and Fulfillment of Life with
               Considerations of the Use of Time in OLD
               Age. Vita Humana 4:129-133.

Burgess, Ernest W.

1954   Social Relations, Activities and Person-
               al Adjustment. American Journal of
               Sociology 59 (4) 352-360.

1960   Family Structure and Relationships. In
               Aging in Western Society. E. Burgess Ed.
               Chicago: University of Chicago Press.

Byrne, Susan W.

1974   Arden, An Adult Community. In Anthro-
               pologists in Cities. G. Foster and R.
               Kemper Eds. Boston: Little, Brown and
               Co.

Carp, Frances M.

1968   Effects of Improved Housing on the Lives
               of Older People. In Middle Age and
               Aging: A Reader in Social Psychology.
               B. Neugarten Ed. Chicago and London:
               University of Chicago Press. Pp. 409-
               416.

Cath, Stanley H.

1975   The Orchestration of Disengagement. In-
               ternational Journal of Aging and Human
               Development. 6(3)

Clark, Margaret

1968   The Anthropology of Aging. In Middle
               Age and Aging: A Reader in Social
               Psychology. B. Neugarten Ed. Chicago
               and London: University of Chicago Press.
               Pp. 433-443

Cumming, Elaine

1961   Growing Old: The Process of Disengage-
               ment. With William H. Henry. New York:
               Basic Books Inc.

1975   Engagement with an Old Theory. Inter-
               national Journal of Aging and Human
               Development 6 (3).

Developments in Aging: 1974 and January-April 1975

1975   A Report of the Special Committee on
               Aging. United States Senate. Washing-
               ton, D.C.: U. S. Government Printing
               Office.

Eggan, Fred

1950   Social Organization of the Western
               Pueblos. Chicago: University of
               Chicago Press.

Engh, Hans

1959   Senior Community, Western Style.
               Geriatrics 14:812-817.

Erikson, Erik H.

1963   Childhood and Society. New York: W.W.
               Norton and Co.

1975   Life History and the Historical Moment.
               New York: W.W. Norton and Co.

Frenkel-Brunswik, Else

1968   Adjustments and Reorientation in the
               Course of the Life Span. In Middle
               Age and Aging. B. Neugarten Ed.
               Chicago and London: University of

Chicago Press.　Pp. 77-84.

Geld, Solomon

1960　　　　Reflections on Group Living of the Elder-
　　　　　　ly.　Geriatrics 15: 579-588.

Glaser, Barney and Anselm L. Strauss

1968　　　　Temporal Aspects of Dying as a Non-
　　　　　　scheduled Status Passage.　In Middle
　　　　　　Age and Aging: A Reader in Social
　　　　　　Psychology. B. Neugarten Ed. Chicago
　　　　　　and London: University of Chicago
　　　　　　Press.　Pp. 520-530.

Goffman, Erving

1961　　　　Asylums: Essays on the Social Situation
　　　　　　of Mental Patients and Other Inmates.
　　　　　　New York: Anchor Books, Doubleday
　　　　　　and Co. Inc.

1963　　　　Behavior in Public Places: Notes on
　　　　　　the Social Organization of Gatherings.
　　　　　　New York: The Free Press.

Gordon, Judith Bograd

1975　　　　A Disengaged Look at Disengagement
　　　　　　Theory.　International Journal of Aging
　　　　　　and Human Development 6 (3).

Harlan, William H.

1954　　　　Community Adaption to the Prescence of
　　　　　　Aged Persons; St. Petersburg, Florida
　　　　　　American Journal of Sociology 59 (4):
　　　　　　332 339.

1968　　　　The Aged in Three Indian Villages. In
　　　　　　Middle Age and Aging: A Reader in Social
　　　　　　Psychology. B.Neugarten Ed. Chicago
　　　　　　and London: University of Chicago Press.
　　　　　　Pp. 469-475.

Havighurst, Robert J.

1954　　　　Flexibility and Social Roles of the
　　　　　　Retired.　The American Journal of

Sociology 59(4):309-311.

1968   Disengagement and Patterns of Aging.
With Bernice Neugarten and Sheldon S.
Tobin. In Middle Age and Aging: A
Reader in Social Psychology. Chicago and
London: University of Chicago Press.
Pp. 161-173.

Hochschild, Arlie R.

1973   The Unexpected Community. Englewood
Cliffs, N.J.: Prentice Hall.

Holter, Paul

1972   Guide to Retirement Living. Chicago,
New York, San Francisco: Rand McNally
& Co.

Homans, George

1951   The Human Group. London: Routledge
and Kegan Paul.

Hoyt, G.C.

1954   The Life of the Retired in a Trailer
Park. American Journal of Sociology 59
(4), pp. 361-370.

Jeffers, Frances and Adrian Verwoerdt

1967   How the Old Face Death in Behavior and
Adaption in Later Life. E. Busse and
E. Pfeiffer Eds. Boston: Little, Brown
and Co. Pp. 163-181.

Johnson, Sheila

1971   Idle Haven. Berkeley: University of
California Press.

Jung, Carl Gustav

1933   Modern Man in Search of a Soul. Trans.
W.S. Dell and Cary F. Baynes. New York:
Harvest Books, Harcourt Brace and
World Inc.

1961   Memories, Dreams, Reflections. New
               York: Vintage Books.

Kleemeier, Robert W.

1951   Effects of a Work Program on Adjustment
               Attitudes in an Aged Population.
               Journal of Gerontology 6.

1954   Moosehaven: Congregate Living in a
               Community of the Retired. American Jour-
               nal of Sociology 59 (4), pp. 347-351.

Klein, Josephine

1956   The Study of Groups. London: Routledge
               and Kegan Paul.

Korda, Michael

1975   Power: Hot to Get It; How to Use It.
               New York: Random House.

Kroeber, Theodore

1966   The Coping Functions of the Ego Mechan-
               isms. In The Study of Lives. R.W.
               White Ed. New York: Atherton Press.

Kropotkin, Peter

1902   Mutual Aid, A Factor of Evolution.
               London: William Heinemann.

Kuhn, Manford H.

1972   The Reference Group Reconsidered. In
               Symbolic Interaxtion: A Reader in
               Social Psychology. J.G. Manis and B.N.
               Meltzer Eds. Boston: Allyn and Bacon
               Inc. Pp. 171-184.

Lamme, Lois

1961   New Concepts in Retirement Homes. G.P.
               24: 179-191.

Langford, Marilyn

1962   Community Aspects of Housing for the

Aged. Ithaca, N.Y.: Cornell University Press.

Lieberman, Morton A.

1968   Psychological Correlates of Impending Death, Some Preliminary Observations. In Middle Age and Aging: A Reader in Social Psychology. B. Neugarten Ed. Chicago and London: University of Chicago Press. Pp. 509-519.

Linton, Ralph

1940   A Neglected Aspect of Social Organization. American Journal of Sociology 45: 870-886.

Maslow, Abraham H.

1943   A Theory of Human Motivation. Psychological Review 50: 370-396.

Masson, Noverre

1972   The National Directory of Retirement Residences. New York: Frederick Fell.

Mills, Theodore and Stan Rosenberg

1970   Readings on the Sociology of Small Groups. Englewood Cliffs, N.J.: Prentice Hall Inc.

Murphy, Lois B. and Alice E. Moriarty

1976   Vulnerability, Coping and Growth, From Infancy to Adolescence. New Haven and London: Yale University Press.

Neugarten, Bernice and Joan W. Moore

1968   The Changing Age-Status System. In Middle Age and Aging: A Reader in Social Psychology. B. Neugarten Ed. Chicago and London: University of Chicago Press. Pp. 5-21.

Norbeck, Edward

1953   Age Grading in Japan.   American Anthro-
                       pologist 55 (3): 373-383.

Owen, Ruth

1958   Campus Living for the Elderly. American
                       Journal of Nursing 58: 1676-1678.

Payne, Raymond

1960   Some Theoretical Approaches of the
                       Sociology of Aging.   Some Forces 38
                       (4): 359-362.

Peck, Robert C.

1968   Psychological Developments in the Second
                       Half of Life.   In Middle Age and Aging:
                       A Reader in Social Psychology. B.
                       Neugarten Ed. Chicago and London:
                       University of Chicago Press. Pp.88-92.

Psathas, George

1972   Ethnomethods and Phenomenology.   In
                       Symbolic Interaction: A Reader in Social
                       Psychology.   J.G. Manis and Bernard N.
                       Meltzer Eds. Boston: Allyn and Bacon
                       Inc. Pp. 125-139.

Riesman, David

1954   Some Clinical and Cultural Aspects of
                       Aging. American Journal of Sociology
                       59 (4): 379-383.

Rose, Arnold and Warren Peterson

1965   Older People and Their Social World.
                       Philadelphia: F.A. Davis Co.

Rose, Arnold M.

1968   The Subculture of the Aging: A Topic for
                       Sociological Research.   In Middle Age
                       and Aging: A Reader in Social Psychology.
                       B. Neugarten Ed. Chicago and London:
                       University of Chicago Press. Pp. 29-34.

Ross, Jennie-Keith

Old Age and Community Formation. Unpub-
lished paper read at the 74th Annual
Meeting of the American Anthropological
Association. December 2-6. San Francisco,
California.

Schutz, Alfred

1974   On Phenomenology and Social Relations.
               Helmut R. Wagner Ed. Chicago and London:
               University of Chicago Press.

Shanas, Ethel

1968   Family Help Patterns and Social Class
               in Three Countries. In Middle Age and
               Aging: A Reader in Social Psychology.
               B. Neugarten Ed. Chicago and London:
               University of Chicago Press. Pp. 296-
               305.

1969   Living Arrangements and Housing of Older
               People. In Behavior and Adaption in
               Late Life. E. Busse and E. Pfeiffer
               Eds. Boston: Little, Brown and Co.
               Pp. 129-149.

Shelton, A.J.

1965   Ibo Aging and Eldership; Notes for
               Gerontologists and Others. Gerontologist
               5 (1): 20-23.

Shibutani, Tamotsu

1972   Reference Groups as Perspectives. In
               Symbolic Interaction: A Reader in Social
               Psychology. J.G. Manis and B. Meltzer
               Eds. Boston: Allyn and Bacon Inc.
               Pp. 160-171.

Simmons, Leo W.

1945   The Role of the Aged in Primitive
               Society. New Haven: Yale University Press

1960   Aging in Preindustrial Society. In
               Handbook of Social Gerontology. C.
               Tibbetts Ed. Chicago: University of
               Chicago Press.

1968   Social Participation of the Aged in Dif-
             ferent Cultures. In Sourcebook in Mar-
             riage and the Family. M.B. Sussman
             Ed. Boston: Houghton Mifflin Co. Pp.414-
             421.

Streib, Gordon F.

1968   Are the Aged a Minority Group? In
             Middle Age and Aging: A Reader in Social
             Psychology. B. Neugarten Ed. Chicago
             and London: University of Chicago Press.

Sussman, Marvin

1968a   Relationships of Adult Children with
             their Parents in the U.S. In Sourcebook
             in Marriage and the Family. M. Sussman
             Ed. Boston: Houghton Mifflin Co.
             Pp. 387-403.

1968b   Kin Family Network: Unheralded Structure
             in Current Conceptualizations of Family
             Functioning. In Miggle Age and Aging:
             A Reader in Social Psychology. B.
             Neugarten Ed. Chicago and London: Univ-
             ersity of Chicago Press. Pp. 247-254.

Talmon, Yonina

1968   Aging in Israel: A Planned Society. In
             Middle Age and Aging. B. Neugarten Ed.
             Chicago and London: University of Chicago
             Press.

Tibbetts, Clark

1954   Retirement Problems in American Society.
             American Journal of Sociology 59 (4)
             301-308.

Townsend, Peter

1963   The Family Life of Old People: An
             Inquiry in East London. London, Reading
             and Fakenham: Abridged Edition, Pelican
             Books.

Williams, Richard H. and Martin B. Loeb

1968   The Adult's Social Life Space and Success-
               ful Aging: Some Suggestions for a Con-
               ceptual Framework.   In Middle Age and
               Aging: A Reader in Social Psychology. B.
               Neugarten Ed. Chicago and London: Univ-
               ersity of Chicago Press. Pp. 379-381.

Young, Michael and Hildred Geertz

1961   Old Age in London and San Francisco.
               British Journal of Sociology 12 (2):
               124-141.